The Courage To M.O.V.E.

MAXIMIZING YOUR MOMENTS
OVERCOMING YOUR OBJECTIONS
VALUING YOUR VISION
EMBODYING YOUR EXTRAORDINARY

by
Ebony Vaughan

Copyright © 2022 Ebony Vaughan

Scripture quotations marked (NIV) are taken from the Holy Bible, New International Version®, NIV®. Copyright © 1973, 1978, 1984, 2011 by Biblica, Inc.® Used by permission of Zondervan. All rights reserved worldwide. www.zondervan.com The "NIV" and "New International Version" are trademarks registered in the United States Patent and Trademark Office by Biblica, Inc.®

Scripture quotations marked (TPT) are from The Passion Translation®. Copyright © 2017, 2018 by Passion & Fire Ministries, Inc. Used by permission. All rights reserved. ThePassionTranslation.com.

Scripture quotations marked (AMP) are taken from the Amplified Bible, Copyright © 1954, 1958, 1962, 1964, 1965, 1987 by The Lockman Foundation. Used by permission.

Scripture quotations marked (MSG) are taken from The Message. Copyright 1993, 1994, 1995, 1996, 2000, 2001, 2002. Used by permission of NavPress Publishing Group.
http://www.navpress.com/

Scripture quotations marked (TLB) are taken from The Living Bible copyright © 1971. Used by permission of Tyndale House Publishers, Inc., Carol Stream, Illinois 60188. All rights reserved.

978-1-7362157-7-7

TABLE OF CONTENTS

Acknowledgements 1
Preface 3
PART I: The MINDSET to M.O.V.E. **5**
   Chapter 1: Time to M.OV.E. 7
   Chapter 2: The Power of Gratitude in Purpose 11
      Choosing Gratitude 11
      Gratitude and Contentment 16
      How to Keep a Grateful Heart 18
   Chapter 3: The Power of Self-Love on Purpose 21
      Self-Discovery 24
      Self-Care 29
      Setting Boundaries 32
      The Grace to Grow 35
      The Power of Silence in M.O.V.E.ment 36
      The Power of Rest in Purpose 40
PART II: The MOTIVATION to M.O.V.E. – A Guide **45**
   Chapter 4: Five Steps to M.O.V.E.ment 47
      Step 1: Diligence 47
      Step 2: Authenticity 49
      Step 3: Accountability 51
      Step 4: Making Decisions 52
      Step 5: Resilience 56
   Chapter 5: The Courage to M.O.V.E. 59
      The Courage to Start Again 63

    The Courage to Lead 66

    The Courage to Communicate 68

    The Courage to Endure a "No" 71

Chapter 6: Spiritual Sight in M.O.V.E.ment. 75

    Seeing God's Vision 75

    Being Seen as God's Original 80

    Seeing through the Eyes of God 84

PART III: The MANDATE to M.O.V.E. 89

Chapter 7: Birthing Your Dream 91

    The Psyche 93

    The Power. 95

    The Passageway 98

    The Passenger 100

    Anxiety and Restlessness in Birthing 102

Chapter 8: Executing Our M.O.V.E.ment. 105

    The Power of Discipline. 105

    The Power of Grit 108

    Eliminating Excuses 112

    The Power of the Follow-Through. 115

Chapter 9: Living Our M.O.V.E.ment 121

    The Power of Our Voice 122

    The Power of Time 126

    Managing Time on Purpose 129

Conclusion 133

Scripture References. 135

Sources 153

About the Author 155

Acknowledgements

I would like to first and foremost thank the Lord for his love and faithfulness toward me. In every detail of my life, I see his sovereign hand, and I am so humbled. I am truly honored that the Lord would use me as a vessel to encourage, empower, and equip his people for purpose. What a tremendous blessing – I get to do what I love every day. Every time I think about this, I am overwhelmed with tears of joy for his eternal call. It is not easy, nor is it a perfect journey for me, but with God, all things work together for my good.

I could not do any of what I do without the love and support of my husband, Vincent Vaughan. He continues to push me into purpose, and I will forever be grateful to him. He is also my personal photographer and business advisor. I truly love this man, y'all. To my heartbeats, Joshua and Jessica, your mother loves you immensely. Thank you for your support always.

To my mother, who is my biggest cheerleader and with me every step of the way. I love you so much and my prayer is that you will have all of your heart's desire as you continue to journey through purpose. I thank God for my brother, Jamar, and all of my family and friends for their continued love, support, and prayers. I am so grateful for their constant encouragement and belief in me. God is so kind to me.

To my prayer warriors, thank you so much for always covering me with prayer. I appreciate you and will never forget your acts of service and love toward me. Through every book, every ministry assignment and business venture, you have been there to pray and bring encouragement. I will forever be grateful.

Finally, I would like to honor my spiritual leaders, Apostle Kenneth Robinson and Pastor Lenyar Robinson. I am so grateful for their powerful teaching, prayers, and impartation over the last seventeen years. Apostle Ken, I thank you for your constant words of encouragement and support. You have no idea just how much they have meant to me in this season of my life. Always know that every word you have imparted, I have kept and will nurture to fulfillment.

PREFACE

So often we find ourselves in very difficult positions, whether as the result of a poor choice, a relationship or something beyond our control. In these times it is so easy for us to look at our situations and think, *it's hopeless*. We begin to doubt or question God's promises for our lives. Have you ever gone through a difficult time and not been able to see yourself recovering? Maybe you thought, *this is the end. Nothing else can be done.* I and many others have fallen into this way of thinking at least one point in our lives, and we lived long enough to eventually see that things can get better.

God's plan for our lives never changes; however, it is up to each of us to develop the courage to show up and to build the character necessary to endure life's challenges and fulfill that plan. Although our poor choices and mistakes have consequence, God is not a god of punishment. He only allows circumstances in the lives of his people to edify, encourage, empower, and equip us for the divine path that he has set before us. Although we don't always see that path or understand our circumstances, we must gain the conviction that God's plan is always to develop us to be better and stronger than we were before. In Romans 8:28 (TPT), it says, **"So we are convinced that every detail of our lives is continually woven together for good, for we are his lovers who have been called to fulfill his designed purpose."**

Now I know you may be saying, "It's not always that easy to think of this when you are in the thick of things and hurting." I get it, but once the smoke has cleared and you have an opportunity to embrace the word of God, you must execute the word of God, to bring transformation, hope, and encouragement to your lives. The scripture says **"every detail of our lives,"** so we know from this that God can use everything that occurs in our lives to develop and nurture us. There is no experience in our lives that will go to waste, as God can use it all to bring himself glory. You may have looked at an area in your life and felt, "I wasted so much time in this. I gave my time to this and I cannot get it back." Maybe you feel that your time was taken from you. Well, I come to say that whatever the situation was, it could be that it brought you different knowledge and a greater conviction and resolve.

Understanding this principle will give us the courage to M.O.V.E. and not remain stuck in a state of disappointment and despair from the pain and challenges of our past. Notice I said *stuck* – it doesn't mean that we won't experience these feelings, but the key is not to stay there longer than we should. When we linger in that state, we run the risk of missing out on the lesson or the blessings that are to come.

Embracing our journey through purpose has everything to do with understanding that although chapters may end in our lives, new ones begin. As long as we are here on this earth, there is an opportunity to grow, develop and fulfill the purpose and plan of God for our lives. A *journey* is an act of traveling from one place to another. We are all traveling through the life that God has given us. We may face many roads, detours, and obstructions, but God is with us through them all.

This book is designed to provide biblically based wisdom and strategies to empower you to overcome every obstacle, slay every giant, and walk in your God-given authority on earth. Our successful journey through purpose requires us to develop a relationship with our heavenly father, renew our minds and execute the word of God to bring transformation and freedom into our everyday lives. As you read this book, my prayer is that you begin to see yourself and your life on a higher level and that you be driven to M.O.V.E.

PART I

THE MINDSET TO M.O.V.E.

CHAPTER 1

TIME TO M.OV.E.

In 2020, in the midst of the coronavirus pandemic, God gave me this powerful acronym as I was preparing to teach my first online course under my brand Triple G Living. The word *move* has always been a part of my journey, since my teenage years. Whenever I faced a difficult challenge, a painful mistake or choice, or a decision to make, I would always say to myself, "Keep it moving, Ebony." This saying has been with me from high school, through college and throughout my spiritual walk and professional career. "Keep it moving" to me means not allowing myself to get stuck, wallowing in my sorrows and defeat, but getting back up and continuing moving forward. However much pain I was in, I would give myself time to cry and complain (not too long), and then I would say, "What are you going to do now?" This is not something I was taught, but something that I just felt was necessary for me to survive.

In 2020, God brought this word back to me with a similar but more powerful meaning. It is not only about surviving, but about being able to gain the mindset, character, and diligence to thrive. M.O.V.E. is so much more than just keeping moving. It's about setting a daily intention to show up as the best possible version of yourself that you can. M.O.V.E. is a mindset and mandate that every spirit-filled believer has as they carry out their God-given assignment on Earth. God has equipped us with all spiritual things needed to thrive on earth and act as conduits of his glory, and it is up to us to create internal and external environments that help fulfill this mandate.

M.O.V.E. stands for **m**aximizing your moments, **o**vercoming your objections, **v**aluing your vision and **e**mbodying your extraordinary. When God gave me this acronym it really propelled me into my season of spiritual and professional movement, and despite any thoughts I have had of stopping or slowing down, it has compelled me to keep going. Let's take a closer look at each letter of the acronym.

Maximizing your moments means that you are choosing to live in the moment and that you strive to be a good steward of that moment. It is about not taking anything for granted and recognizing that every moment you have is part of your journey through purpose. Maximizing your moments is also about striving to show up as your best self intentionally, so that you are able to optimize your life in purpose. It's about understanding that every moment, whether good or bad, can be used to bring God glory through your growth or by being a blessing to his people. Maximizing your moments is about understanding that life is God's gift to you and that how you use your moments truly becomes your worship to him.

Overcoming your objections means transforming your mindset, belief system, and values so that they foster a greater sense of belief in God and in yourself. The more you overcome your internal objections that rob you of your peace and hinder you from operating in your full potential, the more you are able to activate the plan of God for your life. If I had believed the thought I had that said I did not have time to write this book, I would have missed out on birthing this book to inspire others to pursue their purpose. We all have internal objections every day that we must overcome in order to execute the plan of God for our lives. We must learn to silence and reprogram the inner voice, which is tainted by negative experiences, traumas, and disappointment, to begin to believe what God has said about us. Later in the book we will talk about being able to believe what God says about us and possessing the ability to see what he sees. This is key as we overcome our objections. Oxford Languages says that *objections* are "feelings of disapproval or opposition." How many of us right now are opposing God's view of us? How many of us do not approve of what God has predestined for our lives? When I put it that way, you may become defensive and think, "I am not doing that to God." But guess what? Whenever we prevent ourselves from obtaining our dreams or have thoughts and feelings that we are not good enough, we disapprove of what God has approved. We must overcome our objections to become the glory carriers that God desires for us to be.

Valuing your vision enables you to take seriously God's plan to prosper you and use you as a vessel to bless his people. We must value our assignments and intentionally invest in them daily. What is it that God spoke to you concerning? Are you investing in it daily?

Valuing your vision means that you prioritize your assignment and you no longer allow fear and stagnation to prevent you from moving forward. You place your assignment in high regard, you identify it as important, and finally you honor it. Many of us find it easier to value the vision of another before the vision that God gave us. We find ourselves working hard tilling someone else's land, then when it is time to till our own, we are tired and often drained. Does this sound familiar? I want to be clear – valuing your vision doesn't mean that you can't help build the visions of others. We are servants. But how many of us have gotten stuck in the visions of others? We have made permanent something that should have been temporary. We have allowed our focus on the vision of others to distract us, preventing us from obeying God's plan for our lives. All through this book we will be talking about the importance of hearing the voice of God concerning our lives and having the courage to obey. Are you obeying God's plan for your life or are you stuck doing a good thing? Always remember, a good thing is not necessarily a God thing.

Embodying your extraordinary has everything to do with demonstrating the essence, nature, and character of God in all things. Embodying means that we take on the nature of the God who created us. Inside of us is infinite knowledge, creativity, and innovation. To *embody*, according to Oxford Languages, means "to be an expression of or to give a tangible or visible form to an idea, quality, or feeling." When we embody our extraordinary, we allow ourselves to be glory carriers and the divine vessels that God uses to carry out his supernatural plan on earth. Embodying means giving ourselves permission to operate in the authority that God has given us to live in purpose. As spirit-filled believers, we also embody our extraordinary by daily executing the word of God in our lives. As the word says, we become living epistles that are read by all men. This can be deeply intimidating, because it means setting our intentions to look like God daily in our actions and the ways we treat others. It is clear that this cannot be done in our own strength, but is only done through the Holy Spirit, which is the extraordinary that abides on the inside of us. Let's look at Ephesians 2:10 (AMP): *"For we are His workmanship [His own master work, a work of art], created in Christ Jesus [reborn from above—spiritually transformed, renewed, ready to be used] for good works, which God prepared for us beforehand [taking paths which He set], so that we would walk in them, living the good life which he prearranged and made ready for us."* When we choose to embody our extraordinary, we embrace our spiritual transformation and go beyond our humanity into supernatural living.

I believe it's time for us to take the limits off of our lives and live supernaturally and in abundance, the way that God desires. He has completed the work in his people and he is waiting for his children to be activated in the earth. It is time to M.O.V.E.

CHAPTER 2

THE POWER OF GRATITUDE IN PURPOSE

Gratitude is one of the most important virtues, and it is a prerequisite to experiencing true joy and fulfillment. *Gratitude* is defined as having a mindset of thanksgiving and appreciation. According to Dr. Robert Emmons, a leading researcher on the topic, there are three major stages of gratitude: recognition, acknowledgement, and appreciation.

Choosing Gratitude

In the life of a spirit-filled believer, the first of these three stages, recognition, is about verbally acknowledging how good God is and how he has proved to you time and time again that he has you and will never leave you. When we recognize the faithfulness of our heavenly father, we put ourselves in a position enter the second stage of gratitude and acknowledge his goodness. This makes us more prone to speak well of him and to seek him. The more we acknowledge him, the more we come to know him. In the third stage, appreciation, we demonstrate the ability to understand the worth, quality, or importance of God. Demonstrating gratitude creates an environment that can be a source of strength and hope.

When we have gratitude, we show our thankfulness to God and others in our expression, whether verbally, physically, or in acts of devotion and submission. We demonstrate gratitude in our relationships through acts of devotion and submission, at the center of which are yielding and loyalty. Yielding and loyalty in our relationship with God mean giving God all the power to direct things in our lives. When we acknowledge God and his presence, his blessings and his hold on our lives, we demonstrate our trust and total dependence. I believe this warms our God's heart. The Bible says that he inhabits the praises of his people. According to Merriam Webster, to *inhabit* means "to live in and/or occupy." When we live a lifestyle of gratitude by praising our God, we develop spiritual roots and increase our yielding to God, which infuses us with strength and encouragement.

The gratitude that we demonstrate to God is not the same as the gratitude we share with others. However, it is the foundation for what we can demonstrate in our earthly relationships. The stages of gratitude are the same, whether with natural relationships or our relationship with God.

Just like in our relationship with our heavenly father, in our earthly relationships, it is key that we recognize, acknowledge, and appreciate those we love and those who love us. We must acknowledge and verbalize the good in others and be able to build from this. We must not take our loved ones for granted in how we act toward them or the ways we talk to them. Acknowledging our feelings for the people we love and demonstrating them in our actions is a sure way to express gratitude. When we exercise gratitude in our daily lives and relationships, it allows us to focus more on the positive than the negative. It empowers us to maximize our moments by making the best of every moment given to us by God and living them all to the fullest.

CHAPTER 2: THE POWER OF GRATITUDE IN PURPOSE

Displaying gratitude requires the power of your choice daily, whatever the season you are in. The bible says in I Thessalonians 5:18 (AMP), ***"in every situation [no matter what the circumstances] be thankful and continually give thanks to God; for this is the will of God for you in Christ Jesus."*** We understand through this scripture that we should give thanks in all things. This can be difficult, but it can be done. Now let's be real – when we are experiencing pain, we do not always feel gratitude in that moment, and that is okay. Feel the feelings and allow yourself to get through them. Once you are out of that moment, take action and use your power of choice to exercise gratitude.

I read an article years ago that stated that for every negative thought, it takes five positive thoughts to combat it. This five-to-one ratio speaks to the power that negativity has to shape our lives. It is time that we begin to paint the canvas of our lives with gratitude and daily choose to ruminate on God's blessings and goodness instead of on our pain and misfortunes.

As spirit-filled believers, we have housed in these human bodies the Holy Spirit, which is our source of power. It is the only source that can empower us to do things that our minds and emotions won't allow us to do. That's right – the Holy Spirit, if we are yielded, will teach us how to love the way he does. It will guide us into healthier and more productive relationships with others. A quote by MJ Ryan says, "Gratitude helps us love well by keeping us focused on the beauty in our relationship and the person we love." When we choose gratitude, we strengthen our earthly relationships and our relationship with the divine.

Gratitude can determine the trajectory of your life, the course it will follow over time. When we embody gratitude daily, we build hope and encouragement, which empower us to keep moving forward. Life can be tough, and we can be faced with some very painful and traumatic experiences. How we experience and see our pain determines whether or not we have the courage to move past it. The feelings associated with our past traumas and negative experiences should be dealt with and not hidden, so that the trajectory of our lives is not guided by them. Our feelings are temporary and will change over time, and they should not determine our trajectory.

I am going to be honest – gratitude does not remove any pain from our lives. However, it enables us to create a safe and hopeful environment that sustains us as we journey through our painful seasons. We begin to see that there is another day. As days pass, we understand that life goes on. When we see that life goes on, we learn that we can make it. When we see that we can make it, we understand that it can always be worse. When we begin to see that it could be worse, we allow ourselves to see that it just might not be as hopeless as we thought. Once we convince ourselves that it is not as hopeless as we thought, we begin to see that things can change. Maybe we come to see things getting better in our lives, relationships, and future. The days are passing by, and we are still here.

Noticing what we already have can make us feel more positive about our lives and help us to experience joy and freedom daily. When we experience joy and freedom, we are able to maximize our moments, overcome our objections, value our vision, and embody our extraordinary. Here are some of the benefits we can see from exercising gratitude daily:

- It increases our self-esteem. Gratitude can help us feel better about our circumstances, which can lead to feeling better about ourselves.
- It increases positivity. When we are able to see the good in our situations, we open up the possibility of better.
- It increases our mood and our ability to interact with others. When we don't demonstrate gratitude in our relationships, we can be very pessimistic and hopeless. Our pessimism is draining and often crippling to others, because they cannot help us. We fail to appreciate

those around us and isolate others with our lack of satisfaction, even if it's not about them.
- It increases our ability to see our lives realistically. When we look through a foggy or dark lens, our vision can be impaired. Negativity bring darkness and despair.
- It increases our sense of peace and combats anxiety. When we demonstrate gratitude, we are living in the present. We take the time to experience the moment and don't obsess over tomorrow.
- It increases our awareness of God in our lives. When we demonstrate gratitude and praise to God for what and who he is in our lives, we yield to his power and protection. The more we feel protected by God, the more strengthened we become.
- It increases our ability to be problem solvers. When we exhibit gratitude in our professions and pursuits, we allow optimism to guide us to solutions instead of getting stuck in complaints and problems.
- It increases our advancement and mobility in the marketplace. Demonstrating gratitude encourages us to see our growth, which empowers us to continue growing instead of focusing on what we haven't achieved. Gratitude helps us find meaning and purpose in our pursuits.
- It increases our health and leads to improvements in conditions such as high blood pressure, heart issues, gastrointestinal conditions, digestion conditions, weight problems, and many others. Gratitude also helps those who are suffering with mental health issues to take control of their lives and get well again.

Above all, gratitude improves our resilience. In difficult seasons, gratitude is often exactly what we need to create in our lives to get through and continue our journey through purpose. If we can stick in and endure the difficult times, we can make it through to better times. But if we give up too soon, we can miss out on the promises of God. Demonstrating gratitude enables us to hope for the better and not get stuck where we are.

Gratitude and Contentment

Gratitude also helps us to focus on ourselves as opposed to placing our focus on what others have. When we focus on what other people have, we tend to diminish what God has done and is doing in our lives. When we are able to focus on what God is doing in our own lives, we give room for more. Not only that, but we are able to celebrate what God is doing in other people's lives as well.

When we don't walk in a state of gratitude, we can become envious, jealous, and even covetous of others. When we are covetous or envious of others, we experience a feeling of discontent and ill will because of the advantages that we perceive them as having over us. A person who does not practice gratitude daily is often vulnerable to these feelings, especially if they believe that another person has more of an advantage than they do. I Thessalonians 5:18 says, "in everything give thanks." Instead of envying another person's advantages or blessings, posture yourself to give thanks to God for them and be in expectation of the good things that God can do in your life. This guards our hearts against envy or covetousness. Remember, this is something that has to be exercised daily. Gratitude is like a muscle that must be worked regularly.

I Timothy 6:6 (AMP) says, ***"But godliness actually is a source of great gain when accompanied by contentment [that contentment which comes from a sense of inner confidence based on the sufficiency of God]."*** We must learn to be content in all things, a state that we cultivate through gratitude. Now, contentment does not replace ambition. To be content means to be satisfied in the state that you are in, but this does not mean that you cannot strive for more. So often, people make the mistake of believing that contentment means we should not desire more or what is coming next. I believe that this is simply not the case. A person can be satisfied with what God has done in their life thus far and still be in expectation of more great things to come. Let's clear up that misconception and allow ourselves to be content and also to be in great expectation of God's next for our lives.

When we demonstrate the capacity of contentment in gratitude, we also enable ourselves to rejoice with others when their blessings appear to exceed our own. I say *appear* because you can never judge what God is doing in your life by looking at others. There is no comparison to the glory of God that is manifested through each of his children. We all have a purpose and divine assignments. No assignment is better or greater than another. They are what each of us was uniquely crafted for. When we fall into envy, it is self-absorption and self-centeredness at work. These things can nullify our perception of the great things that God is doing in our lives. Envy and covetousness are self-centered thoughts that lead to feeling sorry for yourself because of what you think you don't have. These thoughts often rob you of the opportunity to celebrate and rejoice with others. When we come from a self-centered place, we have a propensity to make moments about others into moments about ourselves. Have you ever experienced this – a time when you should be rejoicing with others and you find yourself thinking about what you don't have and where you are? I've been there and done that. The Bible says in Romans 12:15 (AMP), ***"Rejoice with those who rejoice [sharing others' joy] and weep with those who weep [sharing others' grief]."*** Gratitude is an antidote for envious thoughts, and through exercising gratitude daily, we are able to celebrate and rejoice with others. With practice and intentionality, it can transform the way that we experience God, ourselves, and those in our lives.

How to Keep a Grateful Heart

Gratitude produces hope and great expectation of good and better things to come. When we have grateful hearts, we remain in a constant state of remembrance of the things that we have been able to overcome through our heavenly father. To be in constant remembrance of your journey through pain, trauma, and victory does not lessen your freedom, but it often keeps you humble and able to see God's continual hand in your life. If you think about all the things that you have been through, good and bad, can you confidently say God was with you through it all? Absolutely. Our memories, viewed through a constant lens of gratitude, should give us confidence and serve as a defense to hopelessness when we find ourselves in difficult times.

Here are some tips for exercising gratitude daily:

- Give God thanks through devotion and time in his presence. Thank him for the many blessings he has bestowed upon your life. Think of what and where he has brought you from and give thanks often.
- Keep a gratitude journal. Pray for yourself and others, and give prayers of thanksgiving. You can choose scriptures from the book of Psalms and read them out loud, or you can find books that contain prayers you can recite. For instance, my book *Pursuing the Heart and Mind of God through Prayer: A Servant's Lifeline* includes prayers of thanksgiving that I am confident will bless your life.
- Be an encourager of people and invest in things other than yourself. Be intentional about thinking about and doing things for others. Choose causes that are bigger than you. Sometimes we are too self-focused and oblivious to other people and other needs, which is the breeding ground for self-pity and lack of gratitude. Recognize and acknowledge the good in others. Be intentional about demonstrating God's love to all you come in contact with.

- Change your thinking. Train yourself to reframe your thoughts. For example, if you're thinking, "I am never going to be successful," then say, "I thank God for the gifts and talents he has given me." You see that replacement and reframing?
- Change your language. Death and life are in the power of our tongues. Be very mindful of the words you speak – they form your thoughts, which then form patterns of behavior. Ephesians 4:29 (MSG) says, *"Watch the way you talk. Let nothing foul or dirty come out of your mouth. Say only what helps, each word is a gift."*
- Choose to be hopeful. Create the life you desire by believing, trusting, and being led by God. Hebrews 11:1(AMP) says, *"Now faith is the assurance (title deed, confirmation) of things hoped for (divinely guaranteed), and the evidence of things not seen [the conviction of their reality—faith comprehends as fact what cannot be experienced by the physical senses]."*

Gratitude will have us love the unlovable, appreciate all moments – just not good ones – and value our journey despite the challenges. Gratitude will have us smile when we want to cry. Gratitude has the power to dissolve anger by turning our hardened hearts gentle and affectionate.

Living in a constant state of gratitude helps us to acknowledge our Heavenly Father and enables us to experience his keeping power daily. There is a quote by Louise M. Com that says, "Gratitude is the music of the heart when its chords are swept by the breeze of kindness."

I have one more quote to share with you on the subject, this one by Melody Beattie: "Gratitude unlocks the fullness of life. It turns what we have into enough, and more. It turns denial into acceptance, chaos to order, confusion to clarity" (*The Language of Letting Go*, 1990). Gratitude makes sense of our past, brings peace for today, and creates a vision for tomorrow. I truly believe that this is the reality and shift that we need to make to MOVE – to maximize our moments, overcome our obstacles, value our vision, and embody our extraordinary.

CHAPTER 3

THE POWER OF SELF-LOVE ON PURPOSE

Self-love is one of the most important things we can have as we M.O.V.E. through purpose. When we don't love ourselves, it is often difficult to believe in ourselves or feel that we are worthy of God's best. I believe self-love is a necessity in experiencing a life of purpose and fulfillment. Without it, we often devalue ourselves, seeing ourselves through our failures and not for who God created us to be. We have a difficult time recognizing our strengths and what we bring to relationships. When we struggle with self-love, we often find our value in doing and don't understand the concept of being. Lack of self-love causes us to lack belief in ourselves, which often results in us compromising in our relationships, in our values, and in our expectations of others. We settle for less than we deserve and find comfort in living without a voice.

All of these things can define who we become and what we allow in our lives. As a therapist, I am often asked how one can love oneself. For some, this may be a very easy question, but for those of us who have suffered through trauma, rejection, abandonment, and childhood abuse, it can be much harder. As a result of our pain, we begin to live diminished lives and take on the role of the victim in every aspect of our lives, whether abuse is present or not. It becomes a learned behavior perpetuated in our choices, relationships, and life decisions. We might not even recognize that this is what is happening because it becomes such a part of our thinking and behaving. Our value becomes dependent on how others see us and receive us. When we don't see the value in ourselves, not only do we not see ourselves as good enough, but we also struggle to see others as good enough – or, on the other hand, we might see the good in others and choose not to see it in ourselves.

Self-love is defined by Oxford Languages as "having regard for one's own well-being and happiness (chiefly considered as a desirable rather than narcissistic characteristic)." Looking at this definition, we recognize that self-love enables a person to think of themselves. Those who struggle with self-love often put others before themselves, never really considering their own needs or desires. I did this for years until I realized that I was unhappy. I found myself always sad and unfulfilled in my relationships and endeavors, until eventually I discovered that my happiness was my own responsibility and if I wanted to change things, I had to change. This was a process, and it did not happen overnight. But I set a daily intention to put myself first.

Now, I see in my therapy practice that the terms *self-care* and *self-love* seem to have become the trend... getting your nails and hair done, shopping, spa days, rest, movie nights. Simply doing what you want and giving yourself the permission to enjoy. These are all acts of self-care, but it is imperative that we understand the real work here starts on the inside. It starts by us first acknowledging the lack of love of self and giving ourselves permission to begin to make ourselves a priority by being considerate of our thoughts and feelings. This means changing our mindset concerning ourselves. It means having the courage to truly see ourselves – strengths, weaknesses, and all of who we are. It means learning to embrace all of ourselves and choosing to love.

We do this every day in our relationships. Others have flaws and idiosyncrasies that we do not like, but because we love them and want to be with them, we choose not to focus on those parts of them. This is what we need to do for ourselves. Is that hard? I know it was hard for me to break out of the habit of ruminating on my flaws and failures. We must give ourselves the grace to grow, through a daily practice of gratitude and self-knowledge. We must learn to be kind and patient with ourselves. Give yourself a chance to succeed by believing in yourself. If you're struggling with this, take baby steps and believe in someone else's belief in you until you catch on.

Let's look at the biblical definition of love. I Corinthians 13:4–7 (TPT) says, *"Love is large and incredibly patient. Love is gentle and consistently kind to all. It refuses to be jealous when blessing comes to someone else. Love does not brag about one's achievements nor inflate its own importance. Love does not traffic in shame and disrespect, nor selfishly seek its own honor. Love is not easily irritated or quick to take offense. Love joyfully celebrates honesty and finds no delight in what is wrong. Love is a safe place of shelter, for it never stops believing the best for others. Love never takes failure as defeat, for it never gives up."* Imagine treating yourself that way, and think of how far you could go in your life if you showed yourself this kind of care.

Let's talk about the power that self-love brings in our journey through purpose. When you begin to love yourself:

- You learn to celebrate yourself
- You learn to embrace all of yourself
- You learn to see yourself as enough
- You learn to believe in yourself
- You begin to see yourself as a child of God and not through the lens of your mistakes and flaws

- You begin to value your own thoughts and opinions
- You begin to recognize that you have a voice and it matters
- You give yourself permission to be who you truly are without perfection
- You begin to see the beauty and inherent value you possess
- You begin to set standards in relationships
- Your choices begin to reflect what's best for you
- You strip yourself of the victim mentality and take back your power
- You begin to see hope and not hopelessness

Developing and deepening your relationship with your heavenly father helps in self-love. The Bible says in I John 4:8 (TPT), ***"The one who doesn't love has yet to know God, for God is love."*** The more we know God, the better we are able to love ourselves. Our relationship with our heavenly father helps us to begin to see ourselves through the eyes of our father. This was truly my testimony. It was through increasing my intimate relationship with the Lord that I gained the courage to see all of me and embrace it. Through my relationship and the word of God, he showed me his thoughts toward me, and since then I have been on a journey of aligning my heart and mind with his heart and mind regarding me.

It is so important that we set daily intentions to love ourselves more as we deepen our relationship with the heavenly father. It is truly possible to fall in love with ourselves daily. There is true healing in love, and if we are to M.O.V.E. forward in our lives, we have to be full participants in this journey.

Self-Discovery

We can only have a powerful and authentic life in God and in our journey through purpose when we have a deep and thorough knowledge of ourselves. When we gain knowledge of who we are through the eyes of God, it can give us an unshakeable faith and boldness that allows us to flourish in our assignments. Self-knowledge can feel like a vague, ambiguous idea. Think about it. When you are asked the question, "Who are you?", what do you say? When someone says, "Tell me about yourself," what do you think of? So many people have a difficult time answering these questions. We can go years without being able to answer them. Often, people simply associate who they are with what they do, and they may answer from that perspective, or from the perspective of where they have been – or they may define themselves by their mistakes and failures.

Self-discovery is the key to knowledge of who you are and helps in your journey of becoming. There are some essential things to be aware of in order to gain clarity and confidence on who we are. Let's look at them using the acronym "discover."

Dedicate your life to God. Let him be your source. Get to know him and his plans for your life. In Psalm 139:13a (ESV), the word of God says, *"For you formed my inward parts; you knitted me together in my mother's womb."* Refuse to gain definition and direction from anything outside of God. Choose to be who God says you are. The bible says in Jeremiah 29:11 (AMP), *"For I know the plans and thoughts that I have for you,' says the LORD, 'plans for peace and well-being and not for disaster, to give you a future and a hope."* Choose to discover who you are in God and how and why God created you. Let this define you.

Identify your truth. What do you want to stand for? What do you like and dislike, what are your values, the principles that you desire to live by? Think about what means most to you and what your pursuit of it looks like. Think about what makes you do what you do. What drives you?

Sharpen yourself. The journey of becoming means being committed to growing. Improve yourself. Choose to develop skills. Expose yourself to new things, people, and places that broaden your perspective. Choose to see your life as a journey and not a destination.

Conviction must be your starting point. Hold a firm belief or opinion about something. Your strong personal beliefs will guide who you are, what you do, and your daily living. This conviction must not be altered or changed by anything outside of you. Your conviction defines your actions. It explains your why. Because of this, it is vital for you to know and understand your own beliefs. When a person is not clear on this, they are subject to exploitation, manipulation, and coercion. Make a decision this day who and what your source is and what beliefs guide your life decisions. In Hebrews 10:23 (NKJV), it says to *"hold fast the confession of our hope without wavering, for he who promised is faithful."* It is important to maintain your convictions.

Open yourself. To *open* means to move or adjust something to leave a space, allowing access and view. When people allow themselves to be open, they are not intimidated or frustrated by the differences of others. Instead, they learn to embrace them. Being open means embracing the perspectives of others without the fear that you will lose your own. It also means being willing to fail forward. So many people live in guilt, condemnation, and self-loathing, which prevent them from growing and leave them stuck. Failing forward means that a person can reflect on what went wrong, learn the pricey lessons, and choose to do things differently next time.

Value who you are. Learn to love all of you, not just the good. Embrace it all as you grow into what God has called you to be. See your worth and believe that you are enough. Reject the thought that you must measure up. Identify the principles you would like to live by. As children, we learn our principles from our parents, cultures, and families. However, as adults, we must ourselves choose what means the most to us. Consider yourself special, important, loveable, and created by God. Avoid valuing your worth based on

CHAPTER 3: THE POWER OF SELF-LOVE ON PURPOSE

things outside of you such as prestige, popularity, and prosperity. In I Peter 2:9 (AMP), the Bible says, *"But you are a chosen race, a royal priesthood, a consecrated nation, a [special] people for God's own possession, so that you may proclaim the excellencies [the wonderful deeds and virtues and perfections] of Him who called you out of darkness into His marvelous light."*

Express yourself in a way that is consistent with your true self. Choose not to be a carbon copy of others. I remember as a child, I always felt that I was not good enough or popular enough, and I would find myself trying to act like my friends. I saw them as more popular, more stylish, more effective in communication. So I tried my best to act like them. However, I was a fraud, and those who encountered me could tell that I wasn't who I was trying to be, even at that age. When we pattern ourselves after others, it only leads to unhappiness and inferiority. Why? Because we will never be able to measure up to something that we are not. Your unique expression comes from embracing your personality, style, gifts and talents, and idiosyncrasies and refusing to hide or mimic others. I challenge you today to refuse to hide or diminish that funny-sounding laugh, your own personal style, your particulars that may make you different from someone else. Be okay with being different. The Bible says in I Timothy 4:4 (AMP), *"for everything created by God is good and nothing is to be rejected."* And in Ephesians 2:10 (KJV), it says, *"For we are his workmanship, created in Christ Jesus for good works, which God prepared beforehand that we should walk in them."* Walk out who you are, unashamed and unapologetic!

Reconcile with your flaws, shortcomings, and mistakes. According to Merriam Webster, to *reconcile* is "to accept, settle, and/or to make consistent." It is important that people reconcile themselves with their shortcomings and faults so that they no longer live in denial of what they do or don't have. Often we make attempts to hide our weaknesses, and this only creates double lives, deviances that can destroy us, and denial that prevents us from getting better or finding the help we need. This speaks to character or personality flaws, but it also applies to our work in the world – think of the business owner who does not admit to administrative weakness and insists on doing everything themselves, consequently messing things up continually, instead of being honest with themselves and getting the help they need. The Bible says in Romans 14:22 (AMP), *"The faith which you have [that gives you freedom of choice], have as your own conviction before God [just keep it between yourself and God, seeking His will]. Happy is he who has no reason to condemn himself for what he approves."* Reconciling with our flaws stops the internal battle of self-acceptance and helps us to gain the tools to change our lives. When we are no longer condemning ourselves, we give ourselves permission to feel good about who we are, which in turn helps us to embody our extraordinary.

When a person is able to come to terms with who they are, they obtain power. In this state, God has the perfect environment to manifest himself through them. When a person reaches self-acceptance, their barriers, blockages, and boundaries are destroyed and God is no longer put in a box. A peace enters the person's life. The Bible says in Psalm 72:7 (KJV), *"In his days shall the righteous flourish; and abundance of peace so long as the moon endureth."* I declare this word over you today. In this environment, we can flourish. According to Oxford Languages, to *flourish* means "to grow or develop in a healthy or vigorous way, especially as the result of a particularly favorable environment." You can do this when you live your life on purpose by totally embracing yourself and having a willingness to engage in a process of self-discovery.

Self-Care

When we learn to love ourselves, we learn what it means to practice self-care. It is so important for us to take care of ourselves as we journey through purpose. This means ensuring that we are not just looking after our physical health but also making our mental health a priority. Mental health includes our emotional, psychological, and social well-being. It affects how we think, feel, and act. Mental health is important at every stage of life, from childhood and adolescence through adulthood. Although the terms are often used interchangeably, poor mental health and mental illness are not the same things. A person can experience poor mental health and not be diagnosed with a mental illness. In this chapter, I am not focused on diagnosable mental illness as much as on stress, which often robs us of our peace and keeps us stuck, preventing us from M.O.V.E.ing.

Stress, worry, frustration, unhealthy thinking patterns and mindsets, and failure to heal from past hurts and events can all result in poor mental health. When our mental health suffers, it can lead us to immobility and stagnation, making it much more difficult for us to M.O.V.E. Stress can sap away our ability to experience joy and happiness in our lives, and it is also one of the leading causes of some of our most prevalent medical conditions.

Everyone has stress and goes through difficult periods in their life. In most cases, changing behaviors and thought processes and choosing to let go of things that you cannot control can relieve stress immediately. But if you find that your efforts do not make a difference, then do not hesitate to get the help you need. There is a popular saying: insanity is continuing to do the same things over and over and expecting different results. Recognize when what you are doing is not working.

It is possible to serve God and struggle with mental health issues and/or a mental illness. It is up to you to be honest with yourself and get the help you need. God can heal you and he can also use those whom he has equipped to help in the process. Don't be ashamed to seek the help of a therapist, counselor, medical professional, or clergy member. But remember that clergy do not replace mental health professionals in the case of mental illness and the treatment of it.

I want to provide you with some tools for your self-care survival toolbox. When you have a medical checkup, the first thing the doctors do is check your vitals – your weight, height, blood pressure, pulse, temperature, and respiration. These things are the baseline when you are seen by a doctor. Well, here are some baseline things to consider as you learn to take better care of yourself. Let's use the acronym VITALS as we look at strategies for mental health mastery in daily life.

Value your personal needs – Take care of your emotional and mental well-being. You matter. The Bible says in III John 2 (AMP), *"Beloved, I pray that in every way you may succeed and prosper and be in good health [physically], just as [I know] your soul prospers [spiritually]."* Allow yourself to feel and to be able to articulate what you are feeling. Know that God desires for your soul to be free. Don't suppress your emotions or avoid dealing with them because of fear of what others will think. Give yourself permission to experience positive and negative emotions. Learn how to manage them well. Do not put the happiness of others before your own. Avoid being a people pleaser or a busy body.

Invest time and care in you – Invest in your physical, mental, and emotional health. Make sure you attend annual checkups and address physical symptoms that are out of the norm. Make healthy food choices and monitor your intake of unhealthy choices. Exercise and get the proper rest needed. Remember that God wants you to take care of yourself and not to work yourself to exhaustion – consider Psalm 127:2 (AMP): *"It is vain for you to rise early, to retire late, to eat the bread of anxious labors—for*

He gives [blessings] to His beloved even in his sleep." You do not have to burn yourself out in labor to receive the blessings of God. Make every effort not to overwork yourself.

Time – Respect your time. Learn how to balance personal care, relationships, work productivity, and rest. Don't allow people to intrude upon your time or make commitments for you. What do you spend most of your time doing? Monitor what you spend your time on and whether or not it is healthy for you.

Associations – Monitor your associations. Avoid toxic and unhealthy relationships. Know when to say no to yourself and others. Don't let people suck the life out of you. Learn to preserve your energy by being selective of whom you show up for and when. Know that another person's crisis may not be yours. Avoid being an enabler and doing for others what they can do for themselves.

Live – Allow yourself to live and enjoy life. Seek out hobbies, things that you love to do. Smile often. The Bible says in Proverbs 17:22 (AMP), ***"A happy heart is good medicine and a joyful mind causes healing, but a broken spirit dries up the bones."*** Practice daily gratitude. Stop waiting to find happiness and actively choose it instead. Have knowledge of what you want in life and don't mind pursuing. Avoid living in regret. John 10:10 (AMP) says, ***"The thief comes only in order to steal and kill and destroy. I came that they may have and enjoy life, and have it in abundance [to the full, till it overflows]."*** When we fail to experience joy and this abundant life, we are being robbed of the blessing of God. Let's get into the practice of being intentional with our mental health.

Set boundaries – Caring for ourselves also involves our ability to set healthy boundaries in our lives with others and their affairs. Pursue peace. Try not to worry about things that you cannot change. Choose to live in the moment. Learn the art of forgiveness and letting go.

Setting Boundaries

The final item on our self-care VITALS checklist, setting boundaries, is something that people often struggle with. Particularly when we have fear of speaking our truth, fear of rejection, or difficulty saying no to others, our boundaries can soften or disappear altogether. When we lack boundaries, we diminish the value of our voice and settle for things that we are not comfortable with. Ultimately, we can become frustrated and miserable and feel that we are not valued.

Many of us lack boundaries in our family relationships, friendships, jobs, and/or businesses. We struggle with that powerful two-letter word "no" and instead grudgingly say the three-letter word "yes." Resentment builds up inside us and we wind up masking it, wanting to be looked at as a good person, dependable, and always there to support others. People often say yes at the risk of emotional instability and their needs going unmet. They get in the habit of putting others before themselves. A person who lacks boundaries allows others to make decisions for them, which often results in them feeling powerless and not taking responsibility for their own life. In relationships, those of us who struggle with healthy boundaries make other people happy about us – but part of this dynamic is that we then expect them to make us happy in return. Happiness is a choice that should be made by each individual in the relationship. We cannot allow our loved ones to rely on us for their happiness, and we cannot rely on them for ours.

Emotional and intellectual boundaries protect your self-esteem and ability to separate your feelings from others. When you lack boundaries in these areas, you tend to find yourself enslaved to the opinions of others, negatively impacted by their words and actions and often left feeling bruised and battered. When you feel bruised, you can lose your sense of your own personal values and beliefs. People often struggle with bitterness, lack of trust, and the choices they make, and they lose a sense of responsibility. Examples of emotional and intellectual boundary-crossing are:

- Not knowing how to separate your thoughts and feelings from those of your loved ones;
- Allowing others' moods to influence yours;
- Only being happy when others are happy;
- Wait for others' responses, actions, and/or judgment to determine if you are happy;
- Sacrificing your plans, dreams, and goals in order to please or help others.

Do you set healthy boundaries? Do you consider your needs and wants when helping others? Or do you find yourself pulled into affairs that have nothing to do with you? Do you find yourself giving 150 percent at the expense of your emotional, physical, or mental health? Do you often say yes when you don't want to? Are you preoccupied with the thoughts, feelings, and opinions of others?

I want you to think about these questions, and if you say yes to any, commit to making a change. Commit to setting healthy boundaries with those in your life. I challenge you to no longer put others before yourself when doing so risks your mental or physical health.

Once you decide to set healthy boundaries, difficulties can arise in the dynamics of your relationships, or wherever you begin to set those boundaries. Why? Because your new behaviors may be very different than your old ones, which changes the dynamics. Maybe someone who is used to coming to you for everything can no longer access you. Maybe someone who is accustomed to you always rescuing them financially no longer has you as a security blanket. Always remember you are not responsible for the other person's reaction to the boundary you are setting. You are only responsible for communicating your boundary in a clear and respectful manner. If it upsets them, know that is their problem. Some people, especially those accustomed to controlling, abusing, or manipulating you, might test you. Plan on it, expect it, and remain firm. Your behavior must match the boundaries you are setting. You cannot successfully establish a clear boundary if you send mixed messages by apologizing.

At first, you will probably feel selfish, guilty, or embarrassed when you set a boundary. Do it anyway and remind yourself you have a right to make yourself a priority. Setting boundaries takes practice and consistency. Do not allow guilt and condemnation to prevent you from doing what is right. Resist the urge to backpedal by making apologies for the boundaries you set. Be honest. As you begin to make boundary-setting a habit in your everyday life, take note of the relationships that may require redefining as a result of your change. Choose not to accommodate and protect relationships and roles that no longer serve you.

It is so important that we begin to be honest with ourselves and others about how we are doing. It is important for us to begin to take better care of ourselves by setting healthy boundaries and communicating more openly about our thoughts, feelings, and needs. Our mental health truly does matter.

Our mental health matters. We must take better care of ourselves, and this includes consistently checking our vitals. We must give ourselves permission to unapologetically choose ourselves first. This means learning to recognize the signs and symptoms that indicate that there is something wrong and then doing something about them. We must learn to set healthy boundaries and communicate more openly about our thoughts, feelings, and needs. We can only M.O.V.E. forward in purpose when we learn how to love and care for ourselves daily.

The Grace to Grow

One of the things that can stand in the way on our path to self-love and the space it gives us to M.O.V.E. on our journey is the belief that we are not worthy because we are not perfect. But imperfection never means that we do not deserve self-love. It just means that we are still improving and moving toward our fullest expression of God's plan for us. It means we must give ourselves the space and the grace to grow.

Allow yourself to be a work in progress. The phrase *grace to grow* appears in books, blogs, and so many materials. It is one of the most important things for people to master in order to develop personally, professionally, and spiritually. We often get stuck in spirals of self-doubt and rob ourselves of the opportunity to see and acknowledge how far we have come. When we focus on the negative, we can lose sight of the goodness in our lives.

How many times have you beaten yourself up for a mistake you made, a poor choice, a failed test, a failed relationship? Now don't get me wrong, our feelings are valid and it is okay to feel disappointment for what has not gone right in your life. However, we must be committed to growing forward.

Giving ourselves the grace to grow is also about choosing not to rush into things that we may not be ready for. There have been times in all of our lives when we did not wait for something we wanted but throttled forward before we were prepared and, as a result, we failed. When we give ourselves grace to grow, that urgency softens, and we are more able to wait until we are in the right space to reach our goals before we give them our full effort.

Giving yourself the grace to grow requires a change of focus, mindset, and intention. When we do this, we put a stop to grieving what we don't have and learn to live the best we possibly can with the life given to us. We learn to maximize our moments by allowing ourselves to live in the moment and appreciating the time that we have. Giving yourself the grace to grow is a daily practice that takes patience with self. It requires us to be kind to ourselves, forbearing, forgiving, and most of all to believe in ourselves. When we are patient and kind to ourselves, we overcome those internal objections that are negative and disparaging. This requires us to build on our strengths instead of constantly looking at our shortcomings. We must learn to trust that God has us as we navigate through our journey. As our trust in God increases, we begin to embody our extraordinary. Giving ourselves the grace to grow enables the spirit-filled believer to M.O.V.E. in purpose unapologetically.

The Power of Silence in M.O.V.E.ment

Madeline Plucinska says, "Silence instills courage to face our deepest fears and self-limiting beliefs."

The idea of silence in purpose may sound contrary to courage and movement, but just consider – can there be power in silence? Think about it. How many times have you spoken out of turn, or said things that may have been true but didn't need to be spoken? How many times have you spoken disparaging words to yourself and others and done more harm than good? What about those words you spoke and you wished afterward that you had given yourself a little more time before speaking? What about when you have told others of your dreams and they have discouraged you or created confusion, making you question or even doubt your dream? I think that it is safe to say that we have all done these things at least once – or too many times to count.

When we don't see silence as a powerful force, we run the risk of living noisy lives. And when there is a lot of noise around us and inside us, we tend to drown out what we are really feeling and experiencing, or create smoke screens to conceal it. We become distracted, making us unavailable to hear

God for wisdom and instruction. When we fail to see the power in silence, we tend to damage our relationships and offend others. The power of silence is not about diminishing the value of your voice or muzzling you but about using wisdom to create better results in every area of your life. The Bible says in Ecclesiastes 3:7 (AMP), *"There is a time to tear apart and a time to sew together, a time to keep silent and a time to speak."*

Let's look at instances in which silence has great benefits.

When angry – Proverbs 29:11 (ESV) says, *"A fool gives full vent to his spirit, but a wise man quietly holds it back."* James 1:19 says, *"Let everyone be quick to hear [be a careful, thoughtful listener], slow to speak [a speaker of carefully chosen words and], slow to anger [patient, reflective, forgiving]."* We have to be willing to demonstrate the fruit of the spirit, and if you know that this is a difficult area for you, SILENCE IS GOLDEN. Give yourself time to calm down, think logically through things, and then respond. Remember that it is not about not responding, it is about doing so with a level head. Know thyself.

When planning/building – Proverbs 12:23 (AMP) says, *"A shrewd man is reluctant to display his knowledge [until the proper time], but the heart of [over-confident] fools proclaims foolishness."* Proverbs 17:27 (AMP) says, *"He who has knowledge restrains and is careful with his words, and a man of understanding and wisdom has a cool spirit (self-control, an even temper)."* When we are planning, God is still speaking, giving us strategy for our success. This is not the time to bring more opinions in. We must be intentional about hearing his voice clearly. I am certainly not saying you should not seek wisdom or mentorship. But you have to know when God wants to give you strategy. God's plan and purpose for your life is not up for discussion or debate. Get clarity, get precision, and get moving first. Don't reveal too much too soon. Resist the urge to say things to impress others or reveal what God is doing before time. But work heartily as unto the Lord, not as men pleasers, but being obedient to what God has told you to do.

When waiting/trusting God for manifestation – Psalm 62:5 (AMP) says, **"For God alone my soul waits in silence and quietly submits to Him, for my hope is from Him."** When we are trusting God to manifest, we have to watch what we say. It is normal to experience hopelessness, impatience, fear, and discouragement in our season of waiting, but we have to be careful not to allow our words to create negative internal environments that diminish our faith. Trust God and get in alignment with his word. Place your hope in God.

Above all, we are more apt to remain focused and less likely to be distracted. Preventing distraction is the goal when we are journeying through purpose. We are on assignment and our eyes should be focused on the Lord.

There is true value in our voices – and there is tremendous wisdom and power gained through our silence. Be wise in your use of silence and watch the energy you will save and the peace you will experience.

Silence is such a powerful source of strength, wisdom, and peace. It is in the space of silence that we are able to hear more objectively, more strategically, and more clearly. Many of us tend to mistake a quiet person as weak or passive. We tend to believe that a person who is more vocal is more of a leader and risk taker. It is imperative that we never assume that loud is strong and quiet is weak. Assuming that a person is weak because of their silence is a sure way to bring conflict and confusion in any relationship.

Not every silence is a strength, however. Sometimes we choose to keep quiet in order to avoid conflict, particularly a repeated or ongoing conflict with those in our lives. Have you ever done that? Declared that you are not going to say anything else? Now, this is not necessarily the right way to use the power of silence. Silence is not about avoiding, but about centering our thoughts and aligning with God's way of doing things, so that when we do respond, it is in a way that glorifies God and demonstrates the fruits of the spirit. Demonstrating silence as a spirit-filled believer is about valuing the serenity that comes through seeking God, and it is about embracing and implementing the wisdom and instruction that come through our pursuit.

I am finding that as we learn to value silence, we learn to wait patiently and not be in such a hurry to move. The Bible says in Proverbs 29:20 (MSG), ***"Observe the people who always talk before they think—even simpletons are better off than they are."*** Often when we do not carefully consider our words and speak too soon, we destroy relationships, opportunities, and trust, and we have the potential to create toxic environments. When we do not carefully consider our words, we have a tendency to reveal too much before time, which can hinder our effective execution.

When we set an intention to be silent, we have to find other ways to communicate, which means more often than not that our message will require simplicity. This forces us to organize our thought processes and be very intentional about what we think and what we say. It requires thought. Silence allows us to channel our energies. It gives us the clarity we need to calmly face challenges and uncertainty. Creating daily times of silence can be effective for collecting our thoughts, training our minds, and deciding how we will enter into the day.

Choosing silence is a necessary step for us to grow in our ability to experience God in his fullness. We must train ourselves to experience the three *S*'s – silence, solitude, and stillness. *Solitude* is being alone and/or secluded from others. *Stillness* is the absence of movement, and *silence* is of course the absence of sound. All of these are needed in our pursuit of God, and my prayer is that we will set an intention to listen more intently to God, our source for inspiration, instruction, and illumination. Silence enables the spirit-filled believer to maximize their moments and embody their extraordinary. When we allow for silence, we give ourselves time to gather our thoughts and gain clarity in strategy and direction. When it is too noisy and we are distracted by life, we are often robbed of our moments and struggle to connect with God. Our connection with God and his presence is what helps us to embody our extraordinary.

The Power of Rest in Purpose

Rest is such a powerful aspect of journeying through purpose. Too often, we overlook the power that comes from resting when we are pursuing the purpose of God. Resting enables the spirit-filled believer to cease from their natural efforts and tap into the strength and wisdom of God. Rest has a way of enabling the process of reflection, renewal, and resuscitation – three *R*s that are so important to the spirit-filled believer, and we must be strategic and intentional about each of them.

Let's look at each word a little more closely. *Reflection* is defined in Oxford Languages as a "serious thought or consideration." When we are reflective, we allow ourselves to assess our conditions, whether internal or external, and get clear with ourselves about necessary changes. We gain a better understanding of what has happened and where improvements are needed – if we are being honest, of course.

As a social worker, I often see this term used as a skill. Reflection involves a person reviewing their experiences to help make positive changes for their future practice. It turns their experiences into learning and helps them improve their practice in a way that is right for them. Being able to turn our challenges and changes into learning experiences helps us to grow and prevents us from living in the past and condemning ourselves for things we have allowed that may not have gone well. This is essential for the purpose-driven person, as we cannot allow our past to stand in the way or stop the progression of our future. Instead, it must be a guide and a means for growth and development. Reflection requires our willingness to be vulnerable, and our vulnerability reveals that we don't know everything but are still learning. When we rest, we give ourselves time to reflect. This is a time to stop movement and work, to reflect upon what we have been doing and how we should proceed. This is a time for us to look honestly at what we have been doing to determine if changes are needed.

According to Merriam Webster Dictionary, *to renew* means "to restore to freshness, vigor, or perfection, as we renew our strength in sleep; to make new spiritually, to regenerate; to restore to existence, to revive; to make extensive changes in, to rebuild; an instance of resuming an activity or state after an interruption." In each of these definitions, we see that renewal can mean changing something significantly or starting fresh. And it is okay to do either of these. Sometimes on our journey we become stuck in a pattern and don't always realize that change is necessary; we don't always see that we have lost our freshness or vigor. When this happens it doesn't automatically mean that we should stop what we are doing, but it could mean that it is time to reflect and reconsider.

Renewal becomes particularly important when we get stale. Have you ever experienced this feeling? This is real – when we allow what we do to become more about rituals and checking off boxes in our journey through purpose, we run the risk of losing vigor and freshness. Needing to renew does not mean that what you have been doing was wrong, but it might mean that it is a new season or it is time for a shift. Many of us see the need to shift as failure, and I want to challenge you to change that perspective. Taking time to stop and rest positions us for renewal. When we are working, we don't always take the time to pause, and this is why it is so important to be intentional when it comes to rest. Even though it may feel that you are losing time, you could just be getting your wind back. Renewal restores our freshness; it gives us a second wind to keep moving.

The last *R* is *resuscitate*. This is the action of making something active or vigorous again. It is breathing life back into a person – or spiritually breathing life into a person or a work. We see natural resuscitation in CPR, when someone revives the flow of blood and oxygen to the brain and heart of another by breathing in the mouth in order to save the person's life. Spiritual resuscitation is when we shift the posture of our hearts to allow the Lord to breathe life into us, strengthening us in our journey. John 20:21-22 (AMP) says, *"Then Jesus said to them again, 'Peace to you; as the Father has sent Me, I also send you [as My representatives].' And when He said this, He breathed on them and said to them, 'Receive the Holy Spirit.'"*

God has sent you and me to this world as gifts, and we must always remember that we need his spirit to carry out what he sent us to do. Because we are in human form and we experience humanity, we must draw from the Holy Spirit. It is important to be able to receive CPR in the spirit realm. What's CPR to the spirit-filled believer? Communion, power, and restoration. Through our relationship with the Lord, we are able to experience his power and resilience. We are able to understand our assignment and who it is from. This helps us to keep going despite the pressure. God will always equip us for the assignment. But we must always build into our journey times of reflection, renewal, and resuscitation, through rest.

Do you need to reflect? Is it time for you to be renewed? Where in your life is resuscitation needed? This process helps us to be as I Corinthians 15:58 instructs: *"Therefore, my beloved brothers and sisters, be steadfast, immovable, always excelling in the work of the Lord [always doing your best and doing more than is needed], being continually aware that your labor [even to the point of exhaustion] in the Lord is not futile nor wasted [it is never without purpose]."*

You may ask, "How do I do these things? How do I reflect, renew, and resuscitate?"

First, be willing to stop, be willing to interrupt your rituals and programs, your flows and plans. Even though you are always in pursuit of your goal, even though you have made a commitment, make sure you give yourself times throughout the journey when you halt activity. Just to reflect.

Second, assess. Be willing to evaluate your progress or lack thereof. Are you on the path that God set before you? Or have you veered off? Is a change required? Do you have clarity in your hearing? Sometimes life has a way of making too much noise. It has a way of causing distractions, and we lose sight of what is important to God and his plan. This can be so subtle.

Thirdly, take notes and surrender to God again. Allow CPR to take place. Commune with your father; receive his power. Allow yourself to experience the power of God all over again. The power of the cross and the resurrection of our Lord resulted in us too being able to rise again. As you surrender again, allow yourself to be refreshed. Allow the breath of God to reinvigorate you.

And finally, take action. Get back on the journey, refreshed, renewed, and with new resilience. When we do this, we emerge stronger and wiser; we gain more bandwidth and capacity. We begin to hear clearly and our priorities are reset.

Our Lord rose from the dead, and so can we. Maybe we were not physically dead, but some of us have been walking around dry and without zest. In Ezekiel, God posed a question to the prophet. He asked him, can these dry bones live? He told the prophet in Ezekiel 37:5 (AMP), **"Behold, I will make breath enter you so that you may come to life."** I believe that he wants to bring back to life his purpose, his original plan and promise for our lives, so that we can M.O.V.E. We make this possible through our seasons of rest.

PART II

THE MOTIVATION TO M.O.V.E. – A GUIDE

CHAPTER 4

FIVE STEPS TO M.O.V.E.MENT

Now that we've looked at what M.O.V.E.ment is and how to set ourselves up to succeed in it, let's consider the steps we must take to M.O.V.E. daily in our journey through purpose. These are not the only steps, but I see them as some of the most essential, particularly in developing character and stick-to-itiveness. When we build character in our journey through purpose, we develop capacity, which yields endurance and fruitfulness. When we have capacity, we deepen our stamina, which results in consistent movement in our lives. Let's dive in.

Step 1: Diligence

Every step you take to M.O.V.E. in purpose will involve diligence in your pursuits. *Diligence* is defined by Oxford Languages as "careful and persistent work or effort." It means to be steady, earnest, and energetic. So often we struggle with staying the course or putting in the work that it will take to get something done. As spirit-filled believers, we have been given an assignment and a purpose by God, and everything that we need to fulfill that purpose is already in us. The Bible says in II Peter 1:3 (AMP), *"for His divine power has bestowed on us [absolutely] everything necessary for [a dynamic spiritual] life and godliness, through true and personal knowledge of Him who called us by His own glory and excellence."* So God has given us what we need spiritually. Now we must access the natural through our works. We are activated when we are empowered by the Holy Spirit to act. Knowledge of God gives us access to the heavenlies, and with divine access we are able to bring that power on earth through our obedience and action. It is only through diligently taking action that we bring our goals to fruition.

As always, let's look at the word of God. Mark 1:35-39 (AMP) says, *"Early in the morning, while it was still dark, Jesus got up, left [the house], and went out to a secluded place, and was praying there. Simon [Peter] and his companions searched [everywhere, looking anxiously] for Him, and they found Him and said, 'Everybody is looking for You!' He replied, 'Let us go on to the neighboring towns, so I may preach there also; that is why I came [from the Father].' So He went throughout Galilee, preaching [the gospel] in their synagogues and casting out demons."*

Jesus went away and prayed and then was able to do what his father had sent him to do. And we should do the same – hear and obey. This is true diligence in operation. I am concerned for spirit-filled believers who are powerful in the spirit but hindered and stuck naturally. When this happens, it means there is dissonance somewhere. We have to get to the state where the power we experience in our prayer closet is the same power that shakes off life's shackles to bring us into a place of dominion and freedom naturally. After we have prayed, there must be a conviction and an act of our will to do what we know the Holy Spirit is empowering us to do. Why? Because we believe that he has instructed us to do it. Our faith is demonstrated by what we do. James 2:14 (ASV) says, *"What does it profit, my brethren, if someone says he has faith but does not have works? Can faith save him?"* Verse 24 says, ***"You see then that a man is justified by works, and not by faith only."***

When we don't obey, it brings the question: did we believe? There are many reasons why we don't proceed or move in the direction that God is sending us. Maybe it's because we are unclear, maybe we are wounded or burdened, maybe we are distracted, maybe it is not time. Even as people of faith, we often get distracted with things that are foolish in the eyes of God and not worth our attention. It says in Proverbs 12:11 (AMP), ***"He who tills his land will have plenty of bread, but he who follows worthless things lacks common sense and good judgment."*** Whatever the reason for our lack of movement, we must choose to get into the presence of God to hear clearly and gain strength, get in the word for his wisdom to move, and then move courageously. We must be diligent about taking action. The Bible says that the kingdom of God is not in talk but in power.

Step 2: Authenticity

According to Dictionary.com, *authentic* is defined as "having an origin supported by unquestionable evidence." It is also defined as "not false or copied." As spirit-filled believers, we must give ourselves permission to be who God has created us to be. It is so important as spirit-filled believers that we don't attempt to replicate others and that we commit to being the divine originals that God has created each of us to be. God desires his reflection through our individual and unique expressions because it is in this that he truly gets to show off his work of art. Ephesians 2:10 (AMP) says, ***"For we are His workmanship [His own master work, a work of art], created in Christ Jesus [reborn from above—spiritually transformed, renewed, ready to be used] for good works, which God prepared for us beforehand [taking paths which He set], so that we would walk in***

them, living the good life which he prearranged and made ready for us. " God has divinely prearranged our lives so that his glory can be manifested through his creation. To M.O.V.E. forward on our journey, we must not to limit his hand by attempting to walk in another's shoes or convey a level of expression that was not meant for us. We must abide in our uniqueness and resist any urge to self-loathe.

Self-loathing is extreme criticism of oneself. It may feel as though nothing you do is good enough or that you are unworthy or undeserving of good things in life. We have already talked about the importance of paving the way for our journeys through self-love. Self-loathing is a sure way to block God's voice, presence, and purpose for your life. You might block his voice because of the feeling that you are unworthy to hear from him, or you might assume that there is someone else he would prefer to talk to. But remember Psalm 139:13–15 (AMP): ***"For You formed my innermost parts; you knit me [together] in my mother's womb. I will give thanks and praise to You, for I am fearfully and wonderfully made; wonderful are Your works, and my soul knows it very well. My frame was not hidden from You, when I was being formed in secret, and intricately and skillfully formed [as if embroidered with many colors] in the depths of the earth."*** I want you to know that God took his sweet ol' time creating you and he knows just how precious you are to the world.

You step into authenticity when you allow your true self to be a conduit of God's glory, and when you are true to your assignment. If God told you to go left, go left. If he has assigned you to dominate in the marketplace, don't try to dominate in the church. You can serve in the church or your local assembly, but that does not mean this is where your kingdom assignment is. It is important that we discover our unique assignments in God and obey.

Obey, be authentic in your expression of what God has assigned you, and watch just how blessed and fulfilled your life will be. Often, we make the mistake of attempting to abide in places that we were not created for, where he did not place us, and of going where he did not send us. If you question where God is sending you, get in your prayer closet, or seek the face of the Lord through the word of God and your spiritual leaders and mentors. Allow God to direct your path. God desires us to have abundant lives, but we often miss this promise because we are misplaced or attempting to be something that we are not. Give yourself permission to seek God, hear him, and obey. This is the true authenticity of the spirit-filled believer.

Step 3: Accountability

Once we have committed to diligently moving forward on our journey and holding to our most authentic expressions of self and of God's plans for us, our next step is to be accountable in our pursuits. It is essential that we hear God and obey and not allow external factors to become a diversion or distraction that takes us away from what we have committed to. The Bible says in Romans 14:12 (AMP), ***"So then, each of us will give an account of himself to God."*** In your preparation and pruning season, be sure that you focus on what God has for you to do and not the pursuits of others. Also make sure that you do not fall into a space of victimhood – remember that you are responsible for your own progression. Oftentimes people in our lives may not be as eager as we expect to see us grow or to be active participants in our growth. Be careful not to put your focus on them and what they're not doing. There is an awesome quote by Steve Marabolli: "Take accountability... Blame is the water in which many dreams and relationships drown." It is essential that you keep moving forward and lean into God so that he can provide you with what you need.

    Accountability requires a level of authenticity and integrity. We must have the courage to face ourselves, and this at times can be painful. Hebrews

4:13 (AMP) says, *"And not a creature exists that is concealed from His sight, but all things are open and exposed, and revealed to the eyes of Him with whom we have to give account."* God sees us, even if no one else does, and it is important for us to be honest with ourselves so that we can grow. When we are honest with ourselves and willing to address the challenges in our lives, we please God. Part of taking accountability is having the courage to face yourself.

When we are accountable to ourselves and willing to embrace our journey of growth, we no longer allow our inner selves to weigh us down and hinder our movement. We all have dreams, goals, and aspirations that are just sitting on the shelf and we have not moved forward on them. Accountability means taking responsibility for your personal and spiritual growth as well as your assignment in God. God is so faithful, he is able to make grace abound in all areas of our lives if only we are open and honest with ourselves and him. Remember, God is invested in our future and the fulfillment of the assignments that he has predestined for our lives.

Step 4: Making Decisions

Do you have difficulty making decisions? Do you get stuck? I have found that making decisions can be very challenging, especially when fear, doubt and lack of clarity get in the way. We often struggle with paralyzing questions like *Will I make the right decision? Is God going to be pleased? What will others think? How will my life look?*

As spirit-filled believers, we must get to the point where our relationship and communion with God are so consistent and strong that we learn to detect his voice, direction, and prompting. This is something that we work on over a lifetime and no one has the perfect science to it. But it is important that we be intentional about seeking the Lord in all things. I do not think that there is any decision that is too big or too small to consult God for. The more we consult God in his presence, through his word and in sound counsel, the more accustomed we become to his responding, which helps in our decision making. The more confident we are in our intimacy and communion with God, the more likely it is that we will seek him in our decision making and trust his leading.

Think about a relationship with a significant other. The more you get to know them, the more you learn what they like, what they desire, and what to expect from them. Their actions and responses become more predictable. You start to finish their sentences and anticipate their wishes and thoughts. Well, it's the same way with our heavenly father. We start to anticipate his desire, we start wanting what he wants, we start looking like him, we start sounding like him, the closer we get to him. Can you see it? It says in Psalm 37:4 (AMP), ***"Delight yourself in the Lord, and He will give you the desires and petitions of your heart."*** As we draw closer to him, our hearts begin to curve toward him and our appetites shift from pleasing self to pleasing him. As this happens, our thoughts and decisions begin to reflect his. This is the desire of God – that we be his reflection, demonstrating his essence, nature, and love. The closer we draw to him and the more of a reflection we become, the more courage and confidence it gives us in making decisions. Why? Because our confidence and courage are rooted in the word, his instruction and direction.

Here is a simple road map that can help you when making decisions. By no means am I saying that these are to be followed consecutively or to the tee, but these are not just steps to reflect upon. They are concrete measures you can use right away. As you read these, I want you to ask yourself a question: How do I make decisions?

1. Pray – Activate your faith

    Check your heart and your motives. Identify what you want and why.

    Proverbs 16:2 (AMP): *"**All the ways of a man are clean and innocent in his own eyes [and he may see nothing wrong with his actions], but the* Lord *** weighs and examines the motives and intents [of the heart and knows the truth].*"

2. Sift through your desires and needs to find what's worth pursuing and what isn't

    We often desire things that please us, but are not good for us. These things have a way of leading to distractions and hindrances by our own hand.

    James 1:14–15 (AMP): *"**But each one is tempted when he is dragged away, enticed and baited [to commit sin] by his own [worldly] desire (lust, passion). Then when the illicit desire has conceived, it gives birth to sin; and when sin has run its course, it gives birth to death.***"

3. Seek God's counsel – Gain God's perspective

    Be willing to abandon your way of thinking to prevent yourself from going off track.

    Proverbs 10:17 (AMP): *"**He who learns from instruction and correction is on the [right] path of life [and for others his example is a path toward wisdom and blessing], but he who ignores and refuses correction goes off course [and for others his example is a path toward sin and ruin].***"

CHAPTER 4: FIVE STEPS TO M.O.V.E.MENT

4. Seek counsel from others

   But don't get stuck in seeking out too many people!
   Proverbs 11:4 (AMP): *"Where there is no [wise, intelligent] guidance, the people fall [and go off course like a ship without a helm], but in the abundance of [wise and godly] counselors there is victory."*

5. Gather information – Implications, consequences, and long-term results

   Be careful not to get stuck here either. Explore, gather, and look at examples from people who have walked the path.
   Proverbs 19:2 (AMP): *"Also it is not good for a person to be without knowledge, And he who hurries with his feet [acting impulsively and proceeding without caution or analyzing the consequences] sins (misses the mark)."*

6. Develop a plan

   Activate your faith by implementing what you have heard. Use all the information and counsel you have gathered and the guidance you have received from God to choose the right path. Proverbs 16:3 (AMP): *"Commit your works to the Lord [submit and trust them to Him], and your plans will succeed [if you respond to His will and guidance]."*

7. Believe in your plan

   Stand flatfooted in your decision. Evict doubt and doublemindedness. James 1:6–8 (AMP): *"But he must ask [for wisdom] in faith, without doubting [God's willingness to help], for the one who doubts is like a billowing surge of the sea that is blown about and tossed by the wind. For such a person ought not to think or expect that he will receive anything [at all] from the Lord, being a double-minded man, unstable and restless in all his ways [in everything he thinks, feels, or decides]."*

8. Activate your plan

Resist the urge to procrastinate! You've made your decision – now act on it.

James 2:24 (AMP): *"You see that a man (believer) is justified by works and not by faith alone [that is, by acts of obedience a born-again believer reveals his faith]."*

Step 5: Resilience

Resilience is defined by Oxford Languages as "the capacity to recover quickly from difficulties." Some may define it as mental toughness. It describes a person's capacity to bounce back, their elasticity.

How resilient are you? What's your bounce back like? Do you hold grudges? Is it difficult for you to let go of the past? Is it unbearable to know you have made mistakes and suffered failures?

I challenge you now to break the habit of getting stuck in failures, mistakes, or the pain of your past. Make a commitment to yourself to *feel, fix, free up,* and *flourish*.

Feel means that you allow yourself to experience your own emotions that come from the negative and painful parts of your past. It enables you to take ownership of those experiences and get through them instead of suppressing them.

Fix means that you commit to problem solving and changing your perspective and/or behaviors.

Free up means that you choose to let things go. Try your best not to obsess, to ruminate about things that have already happened. Choose to release yourself and any others involved.

Finally, *flourish* means to "grow or develop in a healthy or vigorous way, especially as the result of a favorable environment," according to Oxford Languages. It's all about cultivating a favorable internal environment that allows you to grow beyond your past and give yourself grace to start again – this time differently.

These four things will help you build resilience. The Bible says in Proverbs 24:15-16 (MSG), *"Don't interfere with good people's lives; don't try to get the best of them. No matter how many times you trip them up, God-loyal people don't stay down long; soon they're up on their feet, while the wicked end up flat on their faces."* From these verses, we understand that as spirit-filled believers, we can get back up again. It's not always easy, but it is doable! We must choose to get back up again. We get back up again through the execution of the word of God in our lives. I charge you to get in the word of God and find out what God has to say about you and your situation. Build your faith and resist the urge to dwell on anything that is the opposite of faith. Drown out the voices in your head that want to rehearse negative scenarios with prayer, praise, and the word of God. Find inspiring readings, videos, and audiobooks that you can keep on repeat. Instead of replaying negative tapes, replace them with faith-filled declarations that line up with what your God has to say about you.

Resilience is key in your journey through purpose. In James 1:12 (AMP), the Bible says, *"Blessed [happy, spiritually prosperous, favored by God] is the man who is steadfast under trial and perseveres when tempted; for when he has passed the test and been approved, he will receive the [victor's] crown of life which the Lord has promised to those who love Him."*

In my book *F.I.G.H.T.*, I talk about God's idea of flourishing and how he desires for us to experience fulfillment and joy in him. When the spirit-filled believer is resilient, they cultivate an attitude, altitude, and atmosphere that causes them to flourish. They flourish because they are convinced and confident of *"this very thing, that He who has begun a good work in them will [continue to] perfect and complete it until the day of Christ Jesus [the time of His return]" (Philippians 1:6 AMP)*.

M.O.V.E.ment requires productivity, fruitfulness, and stamina. All five of these steps incorporate these attributes and must be consistently implemented in our daily lives. This is how we gain the power found in the courage to M.O.V.E.

Deepening our awareness of who we are and what we want will help guide us in our journey through purpose. It will also help us to continue in the necessary work of personal development. There can be no movement where there is no personal growth. It is through personal growth and authenticity that we gain the capacity to experience our heavenly father on a deeper level.

Each of these steps takes awareness, accountability, and continued action as we journey through purpose. We must make daily decisions to show up for ourselves and God. When we do this… that's when M.O.V.E.ment takes place.

Chapter 5

The Courage to M.O.V.E.

"Action is what makes all the difference between who we want to be and who we become."

When we find ourselves in uncomfortable spaces or navigating through our blockages, both internal and external, it is courage that enables us to move forward in our lives despite obstacles and our human tendency to self-sabotage. Courage is defined by Merriam Webster's Dictionary as "mental or moral strength to persevere and withstand danger, fear, or difficulty." It is the willingness to do something that scares you. Courage is one of the most important things to have in your pursuit of purpose. With courage, you gain the capacity to silence your inner critic, stand despite the challenges you face, and move forward despite your feelings. All of these things will enable your success and the reward and crown that come from endurance.

After enough difficult experiences, failures, and disappointments, we all develop an inner critic, and it takes courage to silence it. Having the courage to silence your inner critic means choosing to think differently. It means actively shutting down the blackmailer that hides within your inner voice.

This critic often talks you out of moving forward to pursue your dreams. It tells you that you are not good enough; it tells you that you are not ready or in the right season; it convinces you that someone else can do it better. All these thoughts are paralyzing and can lead you to stagnate. I use the word *blackmail* because thoughts of what you have done in the past can haunt you, making you feel unworthy or even unqualified for what God has for you. Sometimes that inner critic will have you believe that nothing good could possibly happen to you. Any sign of goodness coming your way is met with the inner critic planting mistrust and paranoia. But Psalm 31:24 (AMP) says, **"Be strong and let your hearts take courage, all you who wait for and confidently expect the LORD."**

All these thoughts are limiting beliefs that cause the people of God to choose to live in a diminished state of reality and prevent them from experiencing the fulfillment of their dreams and the very life that God has predestined for them. Being courageous means stepping out of your comfort zone, taking risks despite fear, and having the courage to learn from your mistakes. It takes real courage and humility to admit our poor choices and that we may have hurt people along the way. When we allow ourselves to face the difficulty we have created in our lives, we reduce our likelihood of repeating patterns and can truly make a commitment to get better. Always remember, we will never overcome what we are unwilling to accept or see.

There is a quote by Ashley Hogdson that says, "Strength and courage aren't always measured in medals and victories. They are measured in struggles they overcome. The strongest people aren't always the ones who win, they are who don't give up when they lose." As we overcome our struggles, we must be courageous enough to implement new ways of thinking, behaving, and feeling that line up with our pursuit of God and his purpose for our lives. Philippians 4:13 (AMP) says, **"I can do all things [which He has called me to do] through Him who strengthens and empowers me [to** *fulfill His purpose—I am self-sufficient in Christ's sufficiency; I am ready for anything and equal to anything through Him who infuses me with inner strength and confident peace.]"*

It is important to believe in yourself as you believe in God, accept and embrace the path God has set before you, show up every day despite how you feel, rest when necessary, protect your peace, demonstrate gratitude, work hard, stay on your grind, remain humble, be kind to yourself and others, and keep smiling. This is what courage looks like.

God never promised his people a life with no trouble, no pain, no challenges, but he gave us what we need to overcome all things. He left with us a comforter, advocate, and guide who takes us through every season we encounter, and he gave us his word. With these two things, and our belief in God and in ourselves, we can root ourselves in the courage we need to do the things that frighten us and M.O.V.E. forward on our path in purpose.

We can identify five different types of courage that reinforce the spirit-filled believer on their journey. You may recognize some of these in yourself.

Persevering courage – To be *strategic*, to demonstrate *stability*, to possess a *stick-to-itiveness*, and to *show up* despite the odds. You may be the first in your family or the only person to speak out in your job or your community. This kind of courage often requires you to walk alone. It may require you to remain on the journey even if everyone else has fallen along the way. It helps you to finish what you have started.

Intellectual courage – To being willing to change old and faulty *mindsets* that perpetuate error and poor decision making. Be steady in your *mandate* – don't waver. Feed your *motivation* with positivity, affirmations, and biblical truths. With this kind of courage you are willing to learn, unlearn, and relearn with an open and flexible mind. You learn to be self-aware enough to know that your way of thinking may not be the best.

Spiritual courage – To live with purpose and meaning through God in every area of your life. This courage requires you to trust God and stand on his word and what is right in his sight despite what is acceptable in man's perspective or opinion. This kind of courage causes you to take a stand based on your faith and belief in God's word, and it makes you able to walk alone, no matter how lonely it becomes.

Emotional courage – To give yourself the freedom to feel your feelings honestly without regret, guilt, or attachment. You use this kind of courage in your relationships by being able to express your truth despite how uncomfortable it may make you or others. You don't have to be nasty, disrespectful, or offensive but can share in a way that sheds truth on where you are. You don't act on every feeling, but that does not mean they aren't real to you.

Becoming courage – To give yourself permission to be yourself unapologetically. You learn who you are and no longer choose to dumb yourself down or be invisible and without voice. This is the courage that enables self-love, self-acceptance, and self-belief.

Aristotle once said, "You will never do anything in this world without courage. It is the greatest quality of the mind next to honor." This is a truthful quote, but we also have this treasure that lives inside of us that enables us to do all that we do. II Corinthians 4:7 (AMP) says, *"But we have this precious treasure [the good news about salvation] in [unworthy] earthen vessels [of human frailty], so that the grandeur and surpassing greatness of the power will be [shown to be] from God [His sufficiency] and not from ourselves."* We have such a power working on the inside of us that gives us the ability to stand beyond far more than our natural minds and bodies can endure.

Ephesians 6:10 (TPT) says, *"Finally, be strong in the Lord and in the strength of his might."* Another version of this same text says, *"Be supernaturally infused with strength through your life-union with*

the Lord Jesus. Stand victorious with the force of his explosive power flowing in and through you." God has equipped us with the goods to live this life the way he has ordained. We just need to do things his way. We do things his way by having a relationship and communion with him, developing a hunger and thirst for him, developing an understanding of his heart and mind, and being willing to obey. We must engage in a lifelong pursuit of him and his will. We must seek, find, and embody him wherever we find ourselves – whether in church, in our homes, in our communities, on our jobs, in our businesses, in government, in entertainment, in education, in the economy. Let the power that lives in you infiltrate, influence, and impact the world around you. That is living and moving in courage.

The Courage to Start Again

Starting over is such a very hard thing to do. Maybe you have stepped away from something you started due to transitions in life. Maybe you have experienced failure, or had a change of path in career or business. It can be very intimidating because there is an uncertainty associated with trying something new. We risk embarrassment, shame, and ridicule for trying something and it not working out. We ask ourselves:

Am I too old for this?
Can I do this?
Has my time passed?
What if I fail?
Who's going to believe in me?
What will people think?

Our lives are like road maps. Although there is an ideal route from one point to the next, there are also many other routes that are bound to get you to that same destination. They may take you up hills, through mountains and valleys. They might require more time than the ideal route would have. They may require asking for help and direction along the way. You may need more fuel and the roads may be more abrasive, but guess what? You can still get to where you're going.

When you reflect upon your life, there is no denying that you will realize you have not always made the best decisions. You have come through some very tough moments where you have had to ask yourself, how in the world did I get here? But it is in these moments of reflection we come to realize that through it all God has been faithful to us and with each challenge, his mercy and grace have kept us.

If courage is the ability to do something that frightens us, if it is the strength that arises in the face of pain or grief, then surely courage is exactly what we need when it is time for us to start over. We must be prepared to feel the fear and do it anyway.

The fact that we are still alive and have breath in our bodies is our heavenly father's way of saying, "Get up and start again." Nothing that we experience is meant to destroy us. God uses it all to perfect us and to bring more clarity and wisdom to our lives. It is through God's strength and his amazing grace that he renews, restores, and redirects us on our life journeys, however we got to where we are.

Starting over again takes faith. We must be courageous enough to take that leap of faith and M.O.V.E. When we move in faith, we please our father. When he is pleased, there is a reward for his children. In Hebrews 11:6 (ESV), the Bible says, ***"And without faith it is impossible to please him, for whoever would draw near to God must believe that he exists and that he rewards those who seek him."*** We can receive that reward when we have the courage to start over on the path God has ordained for us. This requires action on our parts, both mental and physical. Faith activated is action. It requires our commitment to do the work. James 2:17 (TPT) says,

CHAPTER 5: THE COURAGE TO M.O.V.E.

"So then faith that doesn't involve action is phony." Action is what makes all the difference between who we want to be and who we become. Our daily actions determine the life that we live. We cannot move forward if we do not put our action where our desires are and get to work.

If the life you are living is not one that you desire or are happy with, have the courage to begin again. Seek God, seek his direction, and obey his voice. If you are not clear what his will is, continue trusting him and moving forward until you get clarity. Eliminate regrets and shame that are holding you back from obtaining the life you want now. This can be done by aligning your thoughts with the word of God to elevate your life. Be willing to do the work. Avoid complaining and comparing. Commit to acting daily on the right tasks that will help you to reach your dreams and goals. Seek the counsel of mentors, spiritual leaders, and trusted guides who will provide advice and direction; however, your ultimate confirmation should come from the Lord. Be willing to chart new territories, learn new things, and meet new people. Be open to God's plan for your life and the resources that he orchestrates to get you to where he would like you to be.

Don't despise small beginnings. Sometimes when we are starting over the biggest hindrance can be our last success. If you are starting something very different from what you have experienced before, be okay with the vulnerability of not knowing and your lack of mastery. Give yourself the grace to grow and resist the urge to compare yourself with others. Do your research, but don't get stuck in the details. Change your language and begin to speak well of your endeavors often. See yourself as new and transformed; see what God sees in you. Choose to live abundantly as God desires for his children. Visualize the dream life that you want to live and choose words of affirmation that support your dream and God's promise.

It is all about obtaining the life that God desires for you. Remember the acronym M.O.V.E., a word that has guided me most of my natural and spiritual life: maximize your moments, overcome your objections, value your vision, and embody your extraordinary. Have the courage within you to declare how your story will end according to the will of the father.

The Courage to Lead

Demonstrating leadership is essential to life in purpose. When we think about leading, many of us automatically think about others following us, and this is accurate when you look at the definition of *leadership*. It is defined by Merriam Webster as "the act of leading a group of people; the ability to influence, motivate, and/or guide others to a common goal." Most of the definitions I have seen do have to do with a person being followed by others. Although I do not disagree with these definitions, I do believe that we must be able to demonstrate effective leadership qualities in our own personal lives. Having the courage to lead in our own lives means that we are willing to be trailblazers; we are willing to keep going even when no one is with us. Having the courage to lead means that we are willing to experience a level of vulnerability by speaking up for ourselves and others and refusing to take a back seat. Some of us love to be in the background. We're comfortable there. This is not because we cannot lead, but because we are evading the responsibility that comes with being in front. We are avoiding conflict, failure, embarrassment, and shame. And we are making sure that we don't attract too much attention.

Having the courage to lead means being willing to stand out from the crowd, to follow the plan of God or what is right. When we do what is right, we please God, but not always man. We gain confidence and cultivate a belief in ourselves and God when we desire to please God more than man.

I once heard an author say, "The greatest courage *isn't* the courage to tell people what to do. It's the courage to tell yourself what to do and to actually follow through and do it!" It can often feel easy to hold other people accountable but much harder to be accountable to ourselves. Being an effective leader in our own lives means we hold ourselves accountable for our dreams and our conduct, as well as the assignment that God has given us. It's not the courage to attempt great things. It's the courage to bring our best selves to daily challenges and opportunities. It means being willing to see ourselves authentically and make the changes necessary. Having the courage to lead means being willing to develop a deep conviction that you will not live your life without obtaining the promises of God. We must be so determined to obtain every promise that God has for our lives that we allow nothing to stop us.

Having the courage to lead also means not waiting for permission. As leaders we don't need permission to do what is right. Often, we wait to be told what to do as opposed to operating in the authority that has been given to us. My motto is, if you are going to lead, lead. Have the courage to make decisions. Get on a side and stay there.

Here are several ways that we can become better leaders in our own lives:

- Set goals for our lives and obtain them
- Lead by example – the Bible says that we are living epistles read by all men
- Be courageous – embrace new challenges and endeavors
- Honor others – find goodness and beauty in everyone and everything
- Be intuitive
- Ask questions
- Do what's right and not what's easy

Demonstrating these qualities in your everyday life will produce a positive and fruitful environment that gives you the courage to lead. God has so much in store for us, if only we believe that he is able to do mighty things in our lives. It is through his spirit we are given the courage to do all things.

The Courage to Communicate

Having courageous conversations with ourselves and others is extremely important as we pursue purpose. This is one area so many of us avoid. We find ourselves dodging arguments, in fear of offending others, too defensive, or always running from conflict. We find ourselves not being honest about our true feelings and saying things to please others, despite the pain we have experienced. Does this sound familiar?

These are habits we have created because we don't believe that we have the capacity to disagree without discord or dissention. Maybe we believe the discussion is too delicate and bringing it up will cause a level of vulnerability that we are not comfortable with. Maybe we have given up, because we have tried in the past to discuss the issue and it did not turn out well.

Whatever the reason we seek to avoid, escape, or ignore these conversations, we must get to a place where we welcome them. This means being able to master our emotions and engage in healthy dialogues with others no matter how difficult they may be. When considering whether it's time for a courageous conversation, ask yourself these questions:

Is it worth it? Do I really care?

Can I handle differing views?

Are my emotions in check?

What are the consequences if I say nothing?

Am I willing to accept these consequences?

In a courageous conversation, everyone has the ability to express their views openly and truthfully, rather than defensively or with the purpose of laying blame. Out of this kind of dialogue emerges a new and shared understanding. Courageous conversations require you to possess the ability to sustain dialogue that brings you and others together and not apart. They are about avoiding presumptions and assumptions; they are about avoiding the tendency to take shots at the other person through accusation and subtle insults. Courageous conversations are genuine and consider both you and those you are engaging in dialogue with.

Here are some things to consider when engaging in these types of conversations:

1. Be honest. If you are not going to be honest, don't even try to approach this conversation. This is not the time to deflect, project, or make excuses. Own your feelings and actions. Don't minimize anything.
2. Be clear on the facts. Sometimes our interpretation and perception are based on faulty information or misinterpretation. The Bible says in Proverbs 18:13 (TPT), *"Listen before you speak, for to speak before you've heard the facts will bring humiliation."*
3. Get rid of the fear and limiting beliefs that stop you from addressing a matter. Deal with the fear of rejection that comes from anticipating that your point won't be received well or that the other people will not want anything to do with you once they hear what you have to say. Don't catastrophize the outcome before you even get to it.
4. Humble yourself. When you don't walk in the place of humility, you tend to focus on being right instead of preserving the relationship. When you are focused solely on you, it can get in the way of your ability to be objective and open to the view of another. You must be willing to think past your own feelings to get to a solution. You must be willing to sacrifice something to gain something better. Shift your internal response from "I don't understand" to "help me

to understand." Then be willing to see through the other person's lens. Be willing to compromise instead of pushing your own agenda. Some of us are too darn bossy, and even when we try to be productive in our communication, we come off as controlling and pushy. Yielding is a great way to build in relationship. It says in Colossians 4:6 (TPT), ***"Let every word you speak be drenched with grace and tempered with truth and clarity."*** We've already talked about the truth and clarity – humbling yourself is the grace.

5. Think about your WHY. What is the purpose of the conversation? Think about the gains not only for you but for others as well. What are the risks in having this conversation, and are the relationship and your WHY worth it? Are you trying to prove a point, or will you actively listen? Be clear on your reason for having this conversation. Having an unclear message can mislead or bring confusion.

6. It's okay to experience discomfort. Again, we often avoid courageous conversations because of the way they make us feel. But being uncomfortable can result in growth and the deepening of a relationship. Resist the urge to run. Be courageous and step up.

7. Work on your delivery. Always start off by communicating why you want to have the conversation, what the issue is that you want to discuss, and how the issue has affected you. Never make accusations about the other person's intent – you don't know their intentions. Instead, make a statement such as "When you did this, I felt..." State a fact, and then describe your response to the fact. Don't blame the other person for your emotions. Own them.

8. Don't expect immediate results. Give yourself and others time to process and make the appropriate changes.

9. Avoid this conversation if you are too emotional. You might need to write your thoughts and feelings out a few times before you

approach it. Make sure you pray and ask God for guidance. The Bible says in Proverbs 15:1–3 (AMP), ***"A soft and gentle and thoughtful answer turns away wrath, but harsh and painful and careless words stir up anger. The tongue of the wise speaks knowledge that is pleasing and acceptable, but the [babbling] mouth of fools spouts folly."***

For courageous communication, we must gain mastery in our ability to manage our emotions and talk productively. When we do this, we are better in our relationships, our responses to others, and walking in love, which is what God desires of us. There are times when we will not get a favorable response, but the result isn't the most important thing. The key is the posture of your heart toward self-awareness and growth. Courageous communication isn't always about getting what we want. It is about demonstrating the essence, likeness, and nature of our heavenly father.

The Courage to Endure a "No"

Have you ever applied for a job that you thought you were qualified for and did not get it? Have you ever entered a competition and did not win? How about that promotion you applied for and were rejected? What about that business you started and it was not as successful as you expected? Have you ever put your all into something and for whatever reason it just did not work out? My answers to almost all of these questions is yes. How about you?

The "no"s that we experience in our lives can make us feel rejected, overlooked, or even unworthy. They often lead to depression, discouragement, hopelessness, and fear. These are such powerful emotions, and they can paralyze people and hinder them from moving forward. People then give up and sabotage their dreams and goals by doing something that can affect their journeys negatively forever. It is so important to understand that a no does not have to be final. A no does not always mean that you are not good enough or never going to get that which you desire. It could just mean that the timing is not right. It could mean that you are not prepared for your desires and you require more growth and development. It could also mean that what you desire is good but not for the place you are in currently.

God has a plan for each of his children and all things are truly working for our good. But we must have the courage to trust God through the process. We must be willing to trust that a no today could be a yes tomorrow. We have to learn to deny the urge to give up or go backwards, and instead must be willing to continue in our pursuits with a determination to never give up. The Bible says in Galatians 6:9 (AMP), ***"Let us not grow weary or become discouraged in doing good, for at the proper time we will reap, if we do not give in."***

Not giving up when you encounter a no is one of the greatest qualities of a victorious believer. It can be a very painful road, but there is truly a reward in the press. Sometimes when we experience rejection, we start to question whether we are doing what we are supposed to be doing; we begin to ask ourselves whether God really told us this was our path. Some of us even begin to doubt that God is with us at all.

I've been there and done that. Twenty years ago, I was preparing to take my social work licensure exam. I took that darn test four times before passing. The three times that I failed, I went into my car and cried my heart out. Each time I questioned myself and my ability to be a mental health clinician. After my second exam, I questioned whether I could even pass it at all. Each time I saw the word "FAIL" on the screen, I froze, because at least two of those times I just knew I had passed. But I made a commitment to myself, because this was standing in the way of my professional movement. I decided I would not stop until I saw "PASS" on that screen. I made the commitment and took the test every three months until I finally passed it.

CHAPTER 5: THE COURAGE TO M.O.V.E.

When I got that license, that certificate went up on the wall even before my actual master's degree. The satisfaction I received from finally gaining that license meant so much more to me than the degree, because of the pain that was associated with the process. The doubt I had battled throughout the journey was no longer important.

I promise you, when you find the courage to trust the journey and embrace both defeats and victories, you come to value your destination more. It says in Ecclesiastes 9:11 (AMP), *"the race is not to the swift and the battle is not to the strong, and neither is bread to the wise nor riches to those of intelligence and understanding nor favor to men of ability; but time and chance overtake them all."* We understand in this scripture that there will always be a reward at the end, but we must be willing to endure time and chance. There is a due season for us all. Only God knows your good season, but remember that God's plan is to give us a future and a hope.

Nothing in life that means anything is going to come without a price paid, seasons endured, and the test of chance and time. But we can find the courage to persevere through our trust in God. There is a song by Andrae Crouch that says, "Through it all, through it all, I have learned to trust God." We must gain a resolve that through it all we will trust and stay on our journey through purpose.

Always remember that God is with you in all seasons, and despite the no's you receive, be prepared to say YES to God's plan for your life. His plan requires us to show up at all times. The Bible says it best in I Corinthians 15:58 (AMP): *"Therefore, my beloved brothers and sisters, be steadfast, immovable, always excelling in the work of the Lord [always doing your best and doing more than is needed], being continually aware that your labor [even to the point of exhaustion] in the Lord is not futile nor wasted [it is never without purpose]."*

CHAPTER 6

Spiritual Sight in M.O.V.E.ment

"It's not what you look at that matters, it's what you see." – Henry David Thoreau

Seeing God's Vision

Visibility is a key element of movement in purpose, and as spirit-filled believers we often misinterpret it. When you hear the word *visibility*, you may think of marketing, promoting, or getting your name out to the masses. All these things are awesome in their proper place in building a business brand. But that's not the meaning I have in mind when I say this topic is crucial on our journey.

When we look at Oxford Language's definition of *visibility*, it has three very powerful meanings. It is "the state of being able to see or be seen; the distance one can see as determined by the light and weather conditions; [and] the degree to which something has attracted general attention and prominence." The ability to see and to be seen is the aspect of the power of visibility I want to talk about here.

Our ability to see the vision and plan that God has for our lives is especially important as we journey through purpose. We often lose this visibility, because we take our eyes off God and place them on ourselves or people and things around us. When we take our eyes off God, not only do we open ourselves to the potential to crash but we also can veer off course by focusing instead on ourselves. Often as we journey in purpose, we have dreams or visions of speaking before the masses, being on stages and platforms, traveling all around the world, and becoming just as famous as people we see on television or social media. These are not bad things to aspire to, but these visions can seduce us and cause an obstruction to our vision. When we are dreaming, we lose present visibility, instead seeing ourselves in a time that has not come yet. We can start to focus more on the thing we dream of and not the source by which all things come to us. We run the risk of losing sight of God and his desire for us.

I am not saying that dreaming is a bad thing. But when we lose sight of God on our journey in purpose, we tend to focus on the wrong things, which makes us ill equipped for the promise.

I want you to ask yourself some questions.

Why do you want to be seen? Why do you want to speak to the masses? Why do you want to be famous and travel all around the world? Why do you desire prestige and prominence? Is it to promote yourself or God? Is it so others can know you, or do you want them to glorify God? Is your desire God's desire?

Everyone one of us must answer all these questions as we journey in purpose. The power of visibility has everything to do with being able to maintain our sight/vision of God. When we focus on God and not the dream:

- We can submit ourselves to God's leading. The Bible says in Galatians 1:10 (NIV), ***"Am I now trying to win the approval of*** *human beings, or of God? Or I am trying to please people? If I were still trying to please people, I would not be a servant of Christ."*

- We maintain a level of clarity on our why and our what – the why is God's divine plan for us, and the what is the vehicle in which you serve to bring him glory. We are all vehicles by which God's glory is carried to earth.

- We maintain substance and stability. A person with substance adds value, demonstrates maturity, and through experience has gained wisdom. Substance is not just about an image that you uphold, but it is about a life well lived and learned from. Stability is consistency in your assignment and purpose. When we lose sight of God, we often go from one thing to the next, never really accomplishing God's plan. God's plan for his people comes with purpose and longevity. His desire to prosper us is not a fly-by-night success, it's not a one-hit wonder or a get-rich-quick scheme. God's purpose for our life is for the long haul and may include many assignments along the way. To fulfill it, endurance, stability, and substance must be our pursuit.

- We avoid falling into the trap of pride. Without proper visibility, we can put too much attention on being popular or gaining notoriety instead of on God. The desire to be popular is more than merely wanting others to notice or recognize you. Often when we focus on being popular it becomes an obsession with self. The craving for popularity is part of the spirit of pride, and as spirit-filled believers, we have to be careful. I John 2:16 (TPT) says, *"For all that the world can offer us—the gratification of our flesh, the allurement of the things of the world, and the obsession with status and importance—none of these things come from the Father but from the world."* It feels good to the ego to consider ourselves popular, and we tend to bask in that feeling rather than deal honestly with ourselves about our own weaknesses. Pride inflates our view of our own importance and blinds us to our true source and the vision that he has for us. Even when the choice to please others does not involve open disobedience to God, pride is always at the heart of the desire for popularity. And God hates pride. I am not saying that there is anything wrong with gaining notoriety, fame, and public favor. These can all be good things; I cannot say this enough. But as spirit-filled believers, we must check our motives and the power of our visibility.

I'm going to tell you a story. In 1997, I was a supervisor and up-and-coming speaker and trainer. I was certain that God had called me to be a speaker, and I was so excited to start this journey. I had zeal because I just knew that this was part of my purpose. So when someone asked me to speak at an awards event at a local university, I jumped at the opportunity. I had ample time to prepare, but every time I went to write my speech, my unlearned self would say, "I am going to speak from my heart." Well, I got to the speaking engagement, got on the stage, and nothing came out. Nothing was coming to me. I tried hard to play it off and came up with something short and encouraging to say, but I was embarrassed and just simply disappointed in myself. I had zeal, I had the gift, but no substance nor experience. That was the first and last time that ever happened to me, and I learned a valuable lesson. My assignment was much more than getting my first shot at speaking. It was about me having an opportunity to bring empowerment, encouragement, and equipping to graduating seniors. After all, the person who asked me to do it asked me because they were inspired by the work I did. However, I made that experience about *my* first time speaking in public, outside of my job and my church, and lost sight of what the opportunity was really about.

In our pursuit to gain visibility in the world or our spheres of influence, we don't always allow ourselves the proper equipping and growth necessary to walk in wisdom and maturity. It is essential that we do not despise or negate the work that God is doing in and through us behind the scenes. God has his way and timing when he moves in our lives. Don't miss his great move by losing visibility. See what God is doing in you and allow him to be your divine strategist. Building a brand, gaining visibility in your niche, and impacting the world are all truly for the glory of God, and they come from God, but make sure you build all of those things on a solid foundation and that your end goal is divine. There are many people who have tremendous influence and millions of followers but are building for themselves and not God. They may be popular, but are they equipped to carry out the vision or assignment that God called them to?

In pursuing your purpose, whatever it may be, do you desire fans or to bring transformation? Does what you do or stand for cause others to be better and become who God has predestined them to be? Whether you are a singer, a comedian, an actor, an athlete, an administrator, a doctor, a minister, an evangelist, a teacher, a prophet, an apostle – whatever your niche or profession – does your light shine and draw people to the one who created you? Are you journeying through purpose with a solid foundation while maintaining your vision? Do you clearly see God and his plan for your life?

When you do the work God called you to, whatever state you are in, God's light will shine so brightly that others will see even if they are not looking. You will gain visibility and experience a sense of fulfillment and joy that comes from above. In Matthew 5:16 (TPT), Jesus told the disciples, ***"So don't hide your light! Let it shine brightly before others, so that your commendable works will shine as light upon them, and then they will give their praise to your Father in heaven."*** This should be the end goal for each of us. When we do this, we gain the ability to see and be seen. This is the true power in visibility.

Being Seen as God's Original

As we grow in grace and in our level of maturity in our assignment and purpose, it is important that we do things as unto the Lord and according to his divine plan for us and not for the applause of man. This is tricky when you are building a brand, because there is so much strategy required to ensure success and public visibility. However, the spirit-filled believer must remember to be intentional about always being seen as God has created them and not as something that they themselves have created to fit into a mold. We are our most powerful selves when we live and prosper with complete authenticity. Being authentic is all about being seen as God's masterpiece and a designer original.

Visibility for the spirit-filled believer means not only seeing God but also presenting themselves to the world as God has intended and fulfilling his ordained assignment and purpose. The Bible says in Colossians 3:1–4 (TPT), *"Christ's resurrection is your resurrection too... Yes, feast on all the treasures of the heavenly realm and fill your thoughts with heavenly realities, and not with the distractions of the natural realm. Your crucifixion with Christ has severed the tie to this life, and now your true life is hidden away in God in Christ. And as Christ himself is seen for who he really is, who you really are will also be revealed, for you are now one with him in his glory!"*

When we understand who we are in Christ and the power we have obtained through our heavenly inheritance, we desire for God to be seen through us. This can only happen when we daily live a submitted and crucified life in Christ. Colossians tell us that we also experienced death, and now as spirit-filled believers, our life is hidden with Christ in God. The power of our visibility lies in becoming a reflection of God's glory on earth. As reflections of our heavenly father, we can dominate and execute the plan of God on earth. We have been given instructions through our assignment on how to reflect God's glory, and it is up to us to manifest. As you see, the more God we experience, embrace, and embody, the more likely others will see him manifested in all our endeavors on earth.

When we truly embody our heavenly father, we become unstoppable in our pursuits. We take on God's agenda and become his manifested glory. But what if you are not in the church – what if you are in the marketplace, or in your community, or on your job? Wherever you are and whatever mountain God has called you to, you can be the manifested glory and gift of God where you stand. According to Oxford Languages, to *embody* means "to be an expression of or give a tangible or visible form to (an idea, quality, or feeling)." Wherever we are, we have the potential to bring the invisible to the visible world. But we must be in submission, in sacrifice, and surrendered to the plan of God for our lives. All these things come as we continue to pursue God and his will for our lives. This is not a perfect journey, but we are perfected as we trust God through our process.

The power of visibility also relates to your passion, power, and pursuit. You must keep clear visibility of your purpose in life and set aside the question of how visible you are to the world. Paul instructed Timothy in II Timothy 4:5 (AMP), **"But as for you, be clear-headed in every situation [stay calm and cool and steady], endure every hardship [without flinching], do the work of an evangelist, fulfill [the duties of] your ministry."** Of course, he was talking to Timothy about being an evangelist, but I believe that this can speak specifically to each of our unique assignments and purposes. As spirit-filled believers, let's choose to remain in our area of calling, remain in that place that we say God has called us to, and work. Regardless of how many people see you, how many likes you have, how many followers you have, how many "good jobs" you get – if God called you to a work, be about your father's business. There will be times in your journey when you feel that no one sees, but Job 34:21 (AMP) says, *"For his eyes are on the ways of a man, and he sees all his steps."* God sees all things.

God is the true power in all that we do. We should be seeking God for our purpose, and as he leads us, we must demonstrate passion and conviction in our pursuit. I want to ask you some questions:

- How committed are you?
- How stable are you?
- Are you consistent in what God has called you to?
- Can you be found diligent in a thing, even if no one is looking?
- Do you get bored easily when you don't get the results you expected quickly enough?
- Can you be trusted to carry out your assignment even without public favor and visibility?

The answers to all these questions are key to your power of visibility and to how that power can support you in your path. We must consistently be found in our assignment and purpose and following God's word of instruction for us. It is so important for the spirit-filled believer to daily cultivate a relationship with God to sense his voice and presence. This is how we can demonstrate stability, longevity, and dependability. I challenge you to reach the conviction that you are not moving until God says so.

Now, in the business world, we tend to stop doing things that are not profitable or don't seem to be of interest to the public. And through a natural lens, this might make sense. But my conviction is that if God tells you to do something, despite what you see in the natural world, you must obey.

CHAPTER 6: SPIRITUAL SIGHT IN M.O.V.E.MENT

God's ideas will always be profitable, but the gauge and timing are controlled by him and not us. Does that mean that you can't evaluate and strategize? Absolutely not. But the most important thing is that you do not abort your assignment or purpose because of how things look to the natural eye. God's timing and ways of doing things do not have to conform to natural business laws and practices. Still, he gives us wisdom and strategy. Yes, God is our divine strategist.

Visibility can help us to M.O.V.E. consistently down the right path, the path that God has chosen for us. Our visibility is our ability to see God in all endeavors and to be seen in the area in which we have been called as the manifested gift and glory of God. Here are some tips to help you to increase the power of your visibility:

1. Be a reflection – John 7:18 (NIV): ***"Whoever speaks on their own does so to gain personal glory, but he who seeks the glory of the one who sent him is a man of truth; there is nothing false about him."*** Let the word of God be your guide and you will grow in your assignment. Demonstrate the character, nature, and essence of God in all that you do.

2. Be a steward – John 3:27 (KJV): ***"A man can receive nothing, except it be given him from heaven."*** To *steward* means to manage or look after. We are stewards of God's blessings and we want to be found faithful by God in all we do.

3. Seek God's timing – Ecclesiastes 3:1 (AMP): ***"There is a season (a time appointed) for everything and a time for every delight and event or purpose under heaven."*** To recognize God's timing, it is so important to increase your sensitivity to God.

4. Demonstrate faith and conviction – Don't bargain with what God has told you to do. Learn the art of waiting. Be anxious for nothing

but await everything in prayer and supplication. With thanksgiving let your request be known to God, and the peace of God that surpasses all understanding will give you rest.

5. Keep your hand to the plow until God says otherwise. Be found faithful by God.

Seeing through the Eyes of God

With the power of visibility, we develop spiritual sight to be able to discern God's presence and movement in our lives as we journey through purpose. We may not think that we are qualified or strong enough for the path that is set before us, but if God has set us upon a path, he has given us everything we need to fulfill his assignment. Our perception of how he has equipped us will determine whether we gain the courage to move forward. Have you ever felt unqualified, even though God's promise was upon your life? Have you ever felt that your challenges were just too great to overcome? Our ability to see ourselves as overcomers and more than equipped to carry out our God-given assignments is an essential component of the power of visibility. The Lord told Samuel in I Samuel 16:7 (NIV), ***"Do not look at his appearance or at the height of his stature, because I have rejected him. For the LORD sees not as man sees; for man looks at the outward appearance, but the LORD looks at the heart."***

In this verse, the Lord was sending Samuel to look for the next king to replace Saul. Age, experience, talent, hierarchy in family/pedigree, looks, and public favor did not determine his appointment to be king. God did. Never forget, despite what you see, God sees more, and it is essential that our sight aligns with his so that we do not miss him in our journey through purpose. Remember all that glitz and glimmer is not God. You must always ask yourself if the road you encounter is a promise or instruction of the Lord. If the answer is yes, then you have to begin to see what is before you the way God sees it. In Numbers 13, Caleb tells the people to pursue battle. The people saw how big and strong the men were before them, and they said, "These people are stronger than us and we are as grasshoppers in their sight." In that moment, the people of God did not possess the sight that God did. They were looking with their natural eyes and not through the eyes of God. If God has placed a burden, assignment, or work inside of you, know that you have all you need to fulfill it, and what you do not have, he will provide along the way.

We must align our vision to God's so that we have the power and courage to daily execute his word and assignment on earth. We must begin to change the narratives of what we see and measure them against the word of God. The narratives that we have created through our natural sight often sabotage our success and lead us to choose the wrong things. The Bible says in Proverbs 29:18 (MSG), **"If people can't see what God is doing, they stumble all over themselves; but when they attend to what he reveals, they are most blessed."**

I want you to think about these questions: Do you judge a book by its cover? Do you often generalize and make assumptions based on your thinking and not God's? Are you often extremely critical of others and quick to shut someone off?

Jesus told the disciples in John 7:24 (AMP), **"Do not judge by appearance [superficially and arrogantly], but judge fairly and righteously."** Often our vision is skewed by our thoughts, beliefs, and values, which may not be based on fact – sometimes they are based instead on negative experiences. We think that we know a person or a situation, but we have sized them up only with our natural sight. Maybe we know a little about people's lives, but we should not be convinced. Don't judge based on what you see. Ask yourself what lens you are looking through.

As spirit-filled believers, although we can see through the eyes of God, we often choose to see through our natural eyes. We choose to look at our circumstances, other people, and obstacles through the lens of our humanity. When we do this, we run the risk of walking in error in our assessments of others, and our mistaken judgements often make the challenges in our lives seem insurmountable. According to Oxford Languages, *insurmountable* means that something is too great to be overcome. When we look through the wrong lens on our journey, our challenges seem bigger than they are. However, when we look at them through the sight of God, we recognize that God is bigger than anything we face. I am certainly not implying that we should never experience fear, because that is a normal part of each of our journeys. But it is essential that we gain spiritual sight and that we remain in a state of trust in our heavenly father.

To trust God means that we don't limit him to our understanding but that we allow him full access and freedom to move in our lives as he sees fit. This is one of the guiding practices to journeying through purpose. To M.O.V.E. requires a deep conviction and faith that enables us to keep going even when we were going to stop. To trust God, we must gain the power of visibility, the ability to see God despite wavering conditions. When your visibility is clear, you are able to remain present, experience thanksgiving, and open yourself up to discovering more about God and his plans for your life. The power of visibility is about the spirit-filled believer becoming more and more spirit-led and not self-led. We can be led by the spirit when we are setting our sights on a heavenly perspective, which leads to us embodying our extraordinary. Here are some tips and things to remember as you gain the power of visibility in your life:

- You gain visibility into the mind of God by deepening your relationship with him, and the single most helpful thing you can do to cultivate a deeper relationship with God and his word is to pray.
- Walk in humility and keep yourself open to God.
- See God in yourself daily. Embrace your power daily. Choose to see the good and don't focus on your weaknesses. Build upon your strengths and let God walk you through your process of maturity.
- Seek the Lord and his plans for your life. See God's vision manifest in your life.
- Choose not to doubt God's ability to manifest through your life because of how the world looks to you, but trust God and gain the capacity to see through his eyes.
- Don't judge people by just what you see. Make attempts to see the best in people. Don't discount anyone, for God has the final answer on us all. See people through the love of the father.
- Always keep sight of the bigger picture (God's plan) and don't get stuck in humanity and its details. Remember, it's about focusing on what God focuses on.
- Set your sight on what is good and light. The energy of putting your focus on something causes that thing to increase. Set your sight upon your many blessings and the love all around you, instead of what is wrong and what you do not wish to include in your life.

There is a quote by Henry David Thoreau that says, "It's not what you look at that matters, it's what you see." We must be intentional about gaining divine sight. I challenge you to check your lens and set your attention to see through the eyes of your loving father. I declare today, according to Ephesians 1:18 (TPT), that ***"the light of God will illuminate the eyes of your imagination, flooding you with light and spiritual sight, until*** *you experience the full revelation of the hope of his calling—that is, the wealth of God's glorious inheritances that is in you."* And then, with that clear visibility into God's plan, you can M.O.V.E. in confidence.

PART III

THE MANDATE TO M.O.V.E.

CHAPTER 7

BIRTHING YOUR DREAM

When we think of birth, we usually think of bringing forth a baby from the womb. But birth isn't only physical – spiritual birthing comes when an individual receives salvation and enters the kingdom of God. When this happens, the person becomes born of the Spirit. Whether natural or spiritual, birthing simply means new life has come. Jesus said to Nicodemus in John 3:3 (AMP), *"I assure you and most solemnly say to you, unless a person is born again [reborn from above—spiritually transformed, renewed, sanctified], he cannot [ever] see and experience the kingdom of God."* In John 3:6 (AMP), Jesus also told Nicodemus, *"That which is born of the flesh is flesh [the physical is merely physical], and that which is born of the Spirit is spirit."* For us as spirit-filled believers, the impetus in all that we do to work toward our dreams, goals, and assignment must come from our spiritual birthing.

Birthing of any form is an act of our heavenly father. To birth is to create, to bring life, to bring substance and existence. When we bring substance and enable something to exist, we can create a work of art, a masterpiece, as did our heavenly father when he created us. As spirit-filled believers we have the ability, through our heavenly father, to create and bring life where there is none.

For years, I did not see myself as creative. I remember saying often that I did not have a creative bone in my body. Today I realize I was saying that because I was comparing myself to what creativity looked like in other people. I now understand that it is impossible for me to "not be creative" if I have the life-giver living within me. I am housed in this earthly flesh, yet as a spirit-filled believer, I can live and walk in the Spirit. This gives me the ability to tap into the infinite imagination of the Holy Spirit living inside me.

The Holy Spirit empowers us to bring life to the area and sphere of influence that he has ordained for us. The creativity that lives inside us is vast and pertinent to the gifts and purpose of God. We must enable the birthing of God's plan through our lives, just as we have experienced the glorious entrance into his kingdom. Many of us stop at the spiritual and natural birth but don't realize that we are pregnant with the vision, valuables, and victory that God has equipped us with for our divine assignment. This is what makes valuing our vision so important, because each of us has a unique promise and plan of God that can only be fulfilled through him. Birthing the vision or dream that God has ordained for our lives requires us to be able to M.O.V.E.

There are four major components of a birthing process: the psyche, the power, passageway, and the passenger. In my research into these four *P*s, I found that they are all essential to a healthy delivery as God intends. I want you to put in front of you that dream, that vision, that assignment, that business, that ministry, that relationship, that healing, that divine connection that you believe God has promised, and I want you to begin to posture yourself in a healthy way to birth. It's time to create and execute a birth plan, so that God's perfect will can be manifest in every aspect of our lives. An amazing thing happens through the birthing process and we glorify God when we execute it. And just like natural childbirth, birthing a God idea requires the four *P*s.

The Psyche

The psyche is defined by Oxford Languages as "the human soul, mind, and spirit." Our psyche determines what we think and what we feel. When birthing a vision, the spirit-filled believer must get to the place where they are able to align their thoughts and feelings to God's thoughts and feelings. Birthing requires conviction, commitment, and a consistent pushing out of the powerful life source, the purpose which God has called each of us to. This requires a firm belief not only in God but in ourselves. Our belief in God and ourselves will enable us to believe in the dream and vision that God birthed in us. When you have a firm belief in something, you cannot be easily moved; you are driven by your belief and will often be unyielding as your faith increases. The Bible says in Daniel 11:32b (KJV), ***"but the people that do know their God shall be strong, and do exploits."***

In natural birth, the right emotional state helps the mother cope with the pain effectively; it helps her tune in to her body and helps guide her to her baby's needs, and it allows the other three *P*s to sync up effectively. In spiritual birth, it is equally important. When our thoughts and feelings are aligned with our belief, we create an environment of faith that helps us to journey in and through our assignments. We come to a resolve not only that what God has promised is his desire for us but that we can achieve it. This resolved condition of our psyche is a crucial part of the birthing process.

When birthing a vision, the dreamer is often plagued by impatience, restlessness, anxiety, loneliness, anger, sadness, hopelessness and a sense of being unqualified. They may sabotage themselves, compare themselves with others, or feel intimidated by their vision. They may ask themselves, "Why me? Do I have what it takes? What will people say? Where I am going to get the money?" The dreamer often feels unworthy, lost, that they are not enough, or that they have made a mistake. All this is the condition of the psyche. These thoughts can be devastating and hinder the birthing process when we are unable to arrest them. Having control of our thoughts and feelings is an art that every spirit-filled believer must master. We need to train our psyche to be in alignment with the word of God. It says in Philippians 4:13 (ESV), *"I can do all things through Christ who strengthens me."* When birthing, choose to believe this word. Choose to believe that your birthing will come to full term and that you will deliver and execute that which God has placed inside of you.

Having a positive psyche in our birthing process will require us to cast down the thoughts that war against our dreams and visions and hold us captive and in fear. The Bible says in II Corinthians 10:4–6 (AMP), *"The weapons of our warfare are not physical [weapons of flesh and blood]. Our weapons are divinely powerful for the destruction of fortresses. We are destroying sophisticated arguments and every exalted and proud thing that sets itself up against the [true] knowledge of God, and we are taking every thought and purpose captive to the obedience of Christ."* Spirit-filled believers must wage war against the sophisticated arguments in our minds that attempt to convince us that we should not birth the dream. When birthing a dream, we must fortify our minds with positive affirmations, faith, truth, and stick-to-itiveness. There's that word again. We must be steadfast and enduring in a thing to receive the promise.

Here are some tips to creating an internal environment of conviction, commitment, and consistency.

1. Know who you are and what God desires you to do. Deal with those thoughts of inferiority and insecurity. Get rid of them by believing what God believes about you!
2. Know God's vision for your life

3. Know your limiting beliefs and destroy them by replacing with belief in limitless possibilities through God. Destroy fear and dead works, those empty and effortless attempts that will never come to fruition. Be willing to fail forward.
4. Know the word of God concerning you! John 10:10 (TPT) says, ***"A thief has only one thing in mind—he wants to steal, slaughter, and destroy. But I have come to give you everything in abundance, more than you expect—life in its fullness until you overflow!"***
5. Know your authority and stop waiting for permission. Be willing to grow past your comfort zone and don't allow other people's opinions to stop you from birthing a God idea. Lose the tendency to seek the approval of others. If God said it, get started.
6. Know the difference between feelings and reality. Just because you feel something, it does not mean that it is fact. Gain control of feelings and train them to be subject to you. Think positively and optimistically. Get rid of cynicism about your dream. Cut the complaining and whining.
7. Know how to fan the flame of God's dream to set yourself a healthy environment. Cultivate the fire and ensure the light does not dim, maintaining your joy and fervor. Don't let anyone take this from you.

These are ways we can develop our psyche to birth the assignment that God has so richly placed in each of us. Create a healthy psyche and you will be able to work with any challenges that may arise with the remaining three *P*s.

The Power

In a natural birth, the power is the contractions of the uterus and the mother's additional efforts when pushing. *Contractions* are defined by Oxford

Languages as "the act, process, or result of making or becoming smaller or shorter and broader." In childbirth, it is contractions of the uterus that push the baby through the birth canal. In spiritual birth, the power is the Holy Spirit. The power that works in us is what enables God's people to birth the dream and his divine plan and promise for our lives.

Ephesians 3:19–21 (AMP) says, *"and [that you may come] to know [practically, through personal experience] the love of Christ which far surpasses [mere] knowledge [without experience], that you may be filled up [throughout your being] to all the fullness of God [so that you may have the richest experience of God's presence in your lives, completely filled and flooded with God Himself]. Now to Him who is able to [carry out His purpose and] do superabundantly more than all that we dare ask or think [infinitely beyond our greatest prayers, hopes, or dreams], according to His power that is at work within us, to Him be the glory in the church and in Christ Jesus throughout all generations forever and ever. Amen."* With these scriptures, we see we must have knowledge of the power that is in us and understand that it is through this power that we are able to accomplish God's plan and assignment on earth. The Holy Spirit enables his people to live and demonstrate his power and glory on earth by birthing his plans into the world.

As kingdom citizens, we have the authority to bring heaven on earth. But to do this we have to acknowledge, access, and activate this power with conviction and courage, which will enable us to experience the fullness of the power that is within us. The Holy Spirit is a gift that kingdom citizens receive at the place of salvation, but experiencing the fullness of this power requires the people of God to have an intimate knowledge of him and an understanding of their authority and access through the word of God.

It is possible to receive salvation and be a good ole Christian but not experience the fullness that God desires for each of his children. Some of us struggle with fear, lack of faith, and clouded spiritual sight, which weakens our pushing, making it much harder for us to birth the dream. Often, the spirit-filled believer experiences salvation and redemption but not prosperity and transformation, which hinders us in birthing our God-given dreams and assignments. God is waiting for many of us to catch this revelation and tap into the power source.

When we don't have the revelation of the power that works in us, the contractions in our spiritual lives are not strong enough to birth what God has conceived in us. Now let's be clear – if the power is not strong enough inside of us, it's not because of our heavenly father but because of us. How much power are you experiencing and activating in your life? The power (the Holy Spirit) is there, but how we connect to it and activate it determines our bandwidth and strength to birth the dream. Through our surrender, submission, and sacrifice, we allow the Holy Spirit to freely push out of us the dream, vision, and assignment that God placed in us while we were in our mother's womb. This power that we have gives us the ability to do all things! This power gives us the strength, stamina, and sustenance to endure the pain of birthing. It enables us to keep going when we want to give up. It gives us courage to face our internal and external giants, and it empowers us to *be*.

In natural childbirth, the contractions can't be too strong or too intense, or fetal distress can occur or the mother can be unable to cope with her contractions without medical intervention. The fetus can go into distress when it doesn't receive enough oxygen through the placenta. *Distress* is defined by Oxford Languages as "extreme anxiety, sorrow, and/or pain." Often in our spiritual birthing process we experience these very same emotions. We can become starved of oxygen or come under too much pressure when birthing our dreams. The oxygen we need here is the life of God that is found in the power. As we are birthing our God-given dreams, goals, and assignments, we must always yield to the power source to prevent us from attempting to do things too fast or on our own, under our own steam. Just as the contractions can't be too strong, our desire to birth a thing must be in alignment with God's will. Sometimes we want to birth something simply because we want it, and our motive and intentions are in the wrong place. We can be out of timing and in our own strength. But just as a mother cannot birth a baby without the help of her contractions, we cannot birth our dreams without the power of the Holy Spirit.

What is it you are birthing? A business, a book, a promotion on the job, a nonprofit, a ministry, an idea that needs to manifest? The Lord is with you, and through the power that worketh in us we can manifest the purpose of God for our lives. We may not all birth at the same time, but my encouragement to you is to get in the face of God to gain clarity about the season God has you in, and when it is time, PUSH.

When your season comes for birthing, lean into your faith to access the power of the Holy Spirit inside you. The Bible says that faith comes by hearing. Examine what you are listening to. Is it the word of God, the spirit of truth, or is it those old tapes of unworthiness and regrets?

Feed your mind with positive, affirming, and faith-filled thoughts. Operate from a place of courage when experiencing fear. Launch out into the deep and see your heavenly father as the preserver. Train yourself to trust God by embracing his truth and cultivating an environment of gratitude.

The Passageway

A *passageway* is defined by Oxford Languages as "a narrow way, having walls on either side, that allows access." In natural birth, the passageway is the pelvis. There are several components of the pelvis and each one needs to be working and moving properly and in synchrony to facilitate a successful birth.

CHAPTER 7: BIRTHING YOUR DREAM

In spiritual birth too, all the components of the passageway need to be working and moving properly. When a believer's faith is small and they struggle with fear, it can cause a level of distress that can impact the successful delivery of their dream, vision, or assignment. When we struggle with fear, we often allow procrastination and feelings of intimidation to stop us from moving forward, causing us to get stuck.

In the natural process of childbirth, the woman's abdominal cavity expands in order to ensure the baby's safe entrance into this world. The same happens in spiritual birthing. We must be willing to expand in our knowledge of who God is in us and our ability to act on what we believe. Our bandwidth must be stretched to enable the birthing of the dream and vision that God has predestined for us. Just as our psyche needs to align with the word of God, likewise our faith and works must be activated. We must cultivate a healthy spiritual birthing canal which includes our internal and external environment; it must be large enough to enable the safe launching of what we are birthing. We must allow elevation in our thinking, expansion of our territories, and the execution of God's plan. Our dreams are bigger than us, and so birthing them requires us to expand.

God is doing something in his people, and we all must get to the place where we hear his voice, sense his movement, and respond with our faith in action. God has a plan to prosper each of us and we must be willing to remove the obstructions in our birthing canal and in our faith that will prevent his perfect will from coming to pass in our lives. Some of the obstructions that can impede spiritual birthing are lack of faith and holding on to things that God said to let go of, whether it be behaviors, thoughts, relationships, or feelings. Be willing to sacrifice them so that you can receive the new. This will enable a successful delivery of the dream for your life.

The Passenger

In the natural birthing process, the passenger is the baby, the fetus. It is the amazing blessing that a mother carries for nine or ten months, if full term. Everyone is in expectation of this tiny gift making its entrance into the world. It is crucial for the passenger to be positioned, nourished, and protected while in the womb.

In spiritual birth, the dream and vision of God for his people is the gift, the baby. The gift will come at the appointed time, and until then, we must nourish it with faith and action, the word of God and stewardship. The dreams that God gives his people require our investment and commitment. The Bible says that we were called when we were in our mother's womb. The dream, the vision, has always been God's plan for us, but how we live our lives and our willingness to hear and obey are key to the birthing process. As spirit-filled believers, we must protect the promise of God for our lives the way a mother protects the fetus inside her. We protect our dreams and assignments through the lifestyles we choose, the thought life we embrace, and the faith we demonstrate.

The lifestyle that we adopt has everything to do with whether or not we are able to successfully bring our passenger into the world. Sometimes the relationships we choose and the decisions we make take us away from God's plan. Have you ever chosen a relationship that was chaotic and toxic and you became so consumed with the emotional turmoil of that relationship that it took you off of the path God had for you? What about that job you took without consulting the Lord – the money looked good, but it consumed your time and left you with no energy to fulfill your dreams and purpose? The Bible says in Proverbs 3:6 (AMP), *"In all your ways know and acknowledge and recognize Him, and He will make your paths straight and smooth [removing obstacles that block your way]."* When

CHAPTER 7: BIRTHING YOUR DREAM

we do not acknowledge God in our decision making, we run the risk of filling our lives with distractions and detours that delay or prevent the healthy delivery of the God-ordained dream for our lives. We can also obstruct the spiritual birthing canal by allowing fear to cripple us. When we are operating in fear in our purpose, we bring displeasure to God and we become stuck. Fear and lack of faith have a way of paralyzing the spirit-filled believer. Hebrews 11:69 (AMP) says, *"But without faith it is impossible to please him: for he that cometh to God must believe that he is, and that he is a rewarder of them that diligently seek him."*

The lifestyle we choose determines the environment in which we are giving birth. If a baby is mispositioned in natural birth, it will have trouble fitting through the birth canal. In the case of birthing the dream that God gave us, if we do not position ourselves in an environment where we are empowered, equipped, and encouraged, we may not find ourselves strong enough to endure our birthing process. The external challenges and obstacles that we often face when birthing a dream can threaten our faith and cause us to abort the dream if we are not strong enough to endure. As spirit-filled believers, we must position our passenger with the word of God, prayer, and acts of our faith. When the passenger is correctly aligned and the environment into which we are birthing is one of strength and faith, we gain the capacity to birth the dream.

God promises that his people will give birth to the plans, visions, and purposes he has given them because he will help them. He has equipped us with all spiritual blessings to obtain the promises, but it is up to us to create the environment for birthing to take place. My prayer is that you have been encouraged, empowered, and equipped through the word of God to help you birth your dream.

Anxiety and Restlessness in Birthing

Anxiety and restlessness often arise when we are in the process of birthing something. We often get a glimpse of the vision and desire the quick manifestation of what we see without waiting for God's leading and guidance. We make the mistake of rushing and trying to make things happen in our strength rather than operating within the frequency and timing of God. But there is a rhythm in God. When we go ahead of God, we run the risk of wasting our time, energy, resources, and money. Then we are disappointed when our efforts don't have the outcome desired. Have you ever been guilty of this? Have you found yourself grinding and toiling, only to end up with failure or no results?

The Bible says in Philippians 4:6 (AMP), *"Do not be anxious or worried about anything, but in everything [every circumstance and situation] by prayer and petition with thanksgiving, continue to make your [specific] requests known to God. And the peace of God [that peace which reassures the heart, that peace] which transcends all understanding, [that peace which] stands guard over your hearts and your minds in Christ Jesus [is yours]."* This is a powerful scripture that gives the spirit-filled believer a supernatural task to trust him. I say supernatural because in our own strength many of us won't be able to do this. But we have to believe by faith that what God instructed us to do, he will bless and multiply. In this scripture, it says that God's peace which reassures our hearts will also stand guard over our hearts and minds. God's peace will act as a shield against thoughts containing worry, doubt, and fear as we decide to trust in him.

We must be patient and persevere in our pursuit of purpose to birth that which God has predestined. It is important for us not to mistake persevering with rushing or attempting to make things happen before their time. It is about remaining on the course that we have been set upon and being willing to do what is necessary to carry it through. Patience requires staying on the path despite challenges and recognizing that if God said it, he has given us the capacity to overcome all the challenges on the way.

In Exodus 4:20, Moses wanted a sign to show the people that God's power was with him, and God simply asked him what was in his hands. God has equipped each of us with the power we need to birth his assignment. Being steadfast, convinced, and diligent with what is in your hand will yield a mighty reward. Don't worry about how your birthing process looks. Just stay submitted with your ear to the voice of God as he leads you.

Here are some tips to help you not get restless in your birthing season.

1. Reframe from looking at others and thinking it can't happen for you. Don't count yourself out, no matter what you don't seem to have. It's easy to get caught up in thinking that everything is a once-in-a-lifetime opportunity or that other people's success means you can't succeed too. But in reality, very few things in life have a limited supply. One thing that is limited, however, is time. And every minute you waste resenting someone else's success is sixty seconds you give away.

2. Don't assume you know someone's journey because you see the fruits of their labor. You do not know the cost of their success. No one has a perfect life. Recognize that other people are working on their own accomplishments. Their achievements don't have to diminish or minimize your own.

3. Don't make judgments on what's fair. You don't always know the whole story – and if you are acquainted with the earthly story, who says you know what God has to say about it? Thinking you deserve more and someone else deserves less is a waste of your time and

energy. Life is not about fairness, and for the kingdom believer, it should be about "thy kingdom come, thy will be done." Accept that God has the final say and you are not in control and focus on the path on which God has set you.

4. Create your own definition of success. Avoid limiting the definition of success to prestige, possessions, and popularity. This is not God's definition. Remember you are not in a race with anyone. Resist the urge to become resentful of others when you realize they're not running the same race as you. In fact, you can celebrate their accomplishments when you view life as an opportunity to cooperate rather than compete.

We must always remember Ecclesiastes 9:11 (KJV), which says, ***"the race is not to the swift or strong but to those who endure to the end."*** It is essential that we be willing to remain in God's timing and resist restlessness. Remaining steadfast in a thing enables us to endure even when it does not come to fruition when we desire. To be steadfast means to be resolute, firm, fast, and fixed. Let's carry our baby (assignment, purpose, and gift) to full term according to God's will for our lives.

CHAPTER 8

EXECUTING OUR M.O.V.E.MENT

Now that we know what to do as we journey through purpose, we must move to the next phase: implementation. So often in life, we gain the knowledge and wisdom but do not implement what we know in our daily lives. Execution is activation, and it is imperative that we be activated in our assignments and purpose. When we daily execute our wisdom and knowledge in our actions, we maximize our moments, stewarding the gift of time given to us by God. According to Oxford Languages, to *maximize* is "to make as large or great as possible." We make our lives greater when we demonstrate discipline, grit, and follow-through in our daily behavior.

The Power of Discipline

Discipline is such a challenging fruit to fully embrace. We often set goals and write down visions, yet lack the follow-through to bring them to pass. It is safe to say that none of us is exempt from this often daunting challenge. Think about that weight goal, that relationship goal, that studying goal, prayer goal, business goal... the list goes on. We often find ourselves desiring things that we have not yet gained the capacity or discipline to fulfill.

This becomes a major distraction in our lives, because we begin to beat ourselves up for not accomplishing what we say we are going to do. If we are honest, we are standing in the way of our own success. *Discipline* is defined by lifehack.org as "the ability to control yourself and to make yourself work hard or behave in a particular way without needing anyone else to tell you what to do." It's about willpower, self-regulation, resolve, determination, and drive. All of these attributes are the perfect ingredients for a disciplined life.

I truly believe that without discipline we suffer, emotionally, mentally, and spiritually. We suffer because we remain in a state of wanting that often leads to depression, frustration, disappointment, and hopelessness. Think about areas in your life where you have failed to activate discipline – how did it make you feel? When you look at the area in your life that is affected, what are the results? When we don't have discipline, we cannot obtain the things we say we want. In Proverbs 13:4 (AMP), it says, ***"The soul (appetite) of the lazy person craves and gets nothing [for lethargy overcomes ambition], but the soul (appetite) of the diligent [who works willingly] is rich and abundantly supplied."*** When many of us think of the word *discipline*, the idea of a parent correcting a child comes to mind, and yes, this is a part of discipline and instruction. But we must get to the stage in our lives when we are able to practice *self*-discipline. There is nothing wrong with having an accountability partner, someone who is able to hold us accountable for what we say we want, but we must get to a place in our walk with God where we reach our goals through our relationship with God. It is imperative that we gain strength in this area of our lives. I Peter 1:13 (AMP) says, ***"So prepare your minds for action, be completely sober [in spirit—steadfast, self-disciplined, spiritually and morally alert], fix your hope completely on the grace [of God] that is coming to you when Jesus Christ is revealed."***

CHAPTER 8: EXECUTING OUR M.O.V.E.MENT

Among the fruits of the spirit that we are to bear as kingdom citizens are self-control and temperance. These fruits provide proof that the spirit of God lives in us. As we increase our discipline, we find we now have a helper who lives on the inside of us and has the ability to strengthen us as we grow and seek him daily. The Bible says in Proverbs 25:28 (MSG), *"A person without self-control is like a house with its doors and windows knocked out."* When we don't have discipline, we rob ourselves of the freedom that God desires for us. Here's an idea for your consideration: that thing in which you are not disciplined, you are a slave to. What do you think – is this true? Really consider it. It is important for us to take control of our lives through the strength of God so that we can experience the abundance God promised his children.

In I Corinthians 9:24–27 (AMP), Paul addresses the church and uses the analogy of athletes and obtaining a goal: *"Do you not know that in a race all the runners run [their very best to win], but only one receives the prize? Run [your race] in such a way that you may seize the prize and make it yours! Now every athlete who [goes into training and] competes in the games is disciplined and exercises self-control in all things. They do it to win a crown that withers, but we [do it to receive] an imperishable [crown that cannot wither]. Therefore I do not run without a definite goal; I do not flail around like one beating the air [just shadow boxing]. But [like a boxer] I strictly discipline my body and make it my slave, so that, after I have preached [the gospel] to others, I myself will not somehow be disqualified [as unfit for service]."* This is a powerful example of empowerment and discipline. In order for us to accomplish the purpose of God for our lives, we must take charge and refuse to allow anything to rob us of freedom. Whatever your purpose is, discipline is one of the ingredients in obtaining the promise. The writer Alan Valentine said something really powerful: "Freedom is born of self-discipline. No individual, no nation, can achieve or maintain liberty without self-control. The undisciplined man is a slave to his own weaknesses."

Let's look at things that we must eliminate from our lives in order to activate self-discipline:

- Actions that go against that which we are progressing toward.
- Appetites that prevent us from achieving our goals. What are the habits, thought patterns, and mindsets that work against the purpose and plan of God for our lives? Whether our goals are personal, professional, or spiritual, we must change our appetites and thinking patterns.
- Associations that do not serve us. It is important to create environments that are conducive to our growth and development. We cannot keep company with those who don't align with our purpose. We must evaluate who has our ears and hearts. Do they need to be removed? What are we listening to? Is it healthy for us? Not everything that is good may be good for us in the season we are in.

As you gain the courage to M.O.V.E., my prayer is that you cultivate discipline in every aspect of your life to enable you to reach your every God-ordained dream and goal. You are destined to WIN.

The Power of Grit

According to Oxford Languages, *grit* is defined as "courage and resolve, and strength of character." A person with grit demonstrates conviction and commitment when in pursuit of their dreams and goals. People with grit don't have a problem working hard, and do not allow their situations and feelings to dictate whether or not they obtain their dreams and goals. Grit has everything to do with sacrifice, stamina, substance, and strength.

Many of us may see grit as a secular idea and one that causes people to rely on themselves and not God. But I believe otherwise. Spiritual grit is rooted in unfailing dependence on our heavenly father despite the pain and challenges that we face. Through the ups and the downs, the rich times and the poor times, the smooth sailing and the tropical storms, the grit we embrace as believers is simply the endurance of our relationship with the Lord, no matter what our situation. The Bible says in Hebrews 12:1-2 (AMP), "***Therefore, since we are surrounded by so great a cloud of witnesses [who by faith have testified to the truth of God's absolute faithfulness], stripping off every unnecessary weight and the sin which so easily and cleverly entangles us, let us run with endurance and active persistence the race that is set before us, [looking away from all that will distract us and] focusing our eyes on Jesus, who is the Author and Perfecter of faith [the first incentive for our belief and the One who brings our faith to maturity], who for the joy [of accomplishing the goal] set before Him endured the cross, disregarding the shame, and sat down at the right hand of the throne of God [revealing His deity, His authority, and the completion of His work].***" Just like this powerful example of the grit of Jesus, we must demonstrate this same level of perseverance and endurance as kingdom citizens. God has given us the power to endure all paths that he has set for us. Our challenges become our opportunity to not give up.

Grit is key not only for accomplishing your goals but in your pursuit of God. Have you ever gone through difficult times and fell off of praying, worshiping, and fellowship? The pain and difficulty became too overwhelming to pray or even to read the word. In these instances in our lives, we allowed our circumstances to rob us of the opportunity to be strengthened and receive direction from our heavenly father. Grit is all about not giving up.

When we perfect our ability to press forward despite challenges and gain a supernatural stick-to-itiveness, there is nothing that we cannot accomplish through God. When we demonstrate grit, we remain in a thing until it is complete; we are in constant remembrance of Jesus and how he remained to finish the assignment that was given to him by his heavenly father.

If we desire success in any area of our lives, whether personal, professional, or spiritual, we must be in a place where we understand the crucial matter of grit and endurance. In Romans 5:3–4 (TLB), it says, *"We can rejoice, too, when we run into problems and trials, for we know that they are good for us—they help us learn to be patient. And patience develops strength of character in us and helps us trust God more each time we use it until finally our hope and faith are strong."* When we have grit, we demonstrate courage, and that courage is what gives us the ability to get past our fears, walk into the unknown, and try something we have never tried before. Grit gives us the ability to stand even when we want to fall. It is what helps us to see past our current situations and tap into the spirit of God on the inside of us that causes us to get through all things. Remember, we are all more than conquerors through Jesus. He has defeated our adversary and now is waiting for his people to gain his perspective. His perspective is that we win. We can do all things through Christ who strengthens us.

The more and more I read the scriptures and the closer I get to God, the more I understand that there is no difference between the meaning of the word *grit* in the secular world and in the kingdom of God. It's all the same thing. Endure hardship as a good soldier; be steadfast and unmovable, always abounding in the works of the Lord. I challenge you to adopt this mindset of the kingdom and allow God to strengthen you through every painful moment, failure, mistake, accomplishment, and success. Let God use you in a way that he has never done before.

Let's look at the word *grit*. I have powerful acronym that I believe will help and encourage you as you are in pursuit of growth and development.

Grow forward. Allow all that you go through, whether good or bad, to help you become a better person. Challenge yourself to see the good or the lesson in a thing before you judge it as negative.

Roll up your sleeves and do the heavy lifting of life. Don't be afraid to go through some things. Don't be afraid to be rejected, to walk alone, to miss the mark sometimes. Don't live in fear but in reverence to God and wisdom. Don't fall into the trap of wanting or looking for accolades and applause; just put the work into your assignment, into your relationship, into whatever your endeavor is. Stay focused on the journey and don't get distracted.

Immerse yourself in the thing that you're in pursuit of. Study it; become a student of it. Get clarity on your purpose. According to Oxford Languages, *immerse* means to "involve oneself deeply in a particular activity or interest." Some of us are not deep enough into the things we should be into. We spend far more time on things that mean so little to God or to ourselves. Being immersed means you allow a thing to become a part of your life and whatever you do. When you do this, your passion will be magnified, and you will begin to excel.

Transcend by going above and beyond where we have ever allowed ourselves to go. Oxford Languages defines *transcend* as "to be or go beyond the range or limits of something." It means to surpass an achievement. To do this, we need the strength of God and an impenetrable grit that causes us to stand in the most difficult and dry lands.

God wants us to take off the limits of our minds, bodies, and spirits and to choose to M.O.V.E.

Maximizing our moments, overcoming our objections, valuing our vision, and embodying our extraordinary requires a level of commitment that can only come through hard work and consistency. This is often one of the biggest challenges in achieving our dreams and goals. How committed are you?

Eliminating Excuses

Excuses can be a real danger in our journey through purpose. An *excuse* is defined by Oxford Languages as an attempt to lessen the blame attaching to a fault or offense. When people make excuses, they often seek to defend or justify a decision they have made. Excuses are such an enemy to our purpose, and we must be intentional about avoiding them at all costs.

When we make excuses, we give ourselves permission to stop moving forward in the purpose for our lives. We sanction disobedience by choosing to believe a lie. These lies can be internal or can come from others. Either way, they are deception. We justify a lack of movement with information that is contrary to God.

Excuses lead to procrastination. We stop M.O.V.E.ing because we have convinced ourselves that we are not ready, we are not good enough, we need to learn more, we need a degree, we need experience, we need help. We often make excuses when we are afraid, when we feel inadequate, and when we don't have the faith to trust God. It is safe to say that no one is exempt from this toxic trait that often robs us of our mobility.

Let's go to the word of God, Exodus 4:10–13 (AMP): *"Then Moses said to the Lord, 'Please, Lord, I am not a man of words (eloquent, fluent), neither before nor since You have spoken to Your servant; for I am slow of speech and tongue.' The Lord said to him, 'Who has made man's mouth? Or who makes the mute or the deaf, or the seeing or the blind? Is it not I, the Lord? Now then go, and I, even I, will be with your mouth, and will teach you what you shall say.' But he said, 'Please my Lord, send the message [of rescue to Israel] by [someone else,] whomever else You will [choose].'"*

Moses made excuses as to why he could not obey God right after God demonstrated his miracles unto him. Moses had receipts that God was with him, yet he did not feel that he was worthy enough to do what God asked him to do, and this angered God. How many of us are like Moses? God has shown up in our lives, he has demonstrated his faithfulness toward us, yet we have been hindered in obeying because of our excuses.

I want to challenge you today – where are your excuses? Excuses make our journey through purpose about us and not God. As spirit-filled believers, we must understand that God's assignment for our lives will always involve his power and purpose. There is absolutely nothing we can do without God's power flowing through us. Our excuses have a way of diminishing God's power and purpose and amplifying our humanity and our frailties. Moses tried to justify his not doing with his lack of eloquent speech. The funny thing was that eloquent speech was not a requirement for him. What excuses are you telling yourself now that are not even a requirement for your purpose? God never asks his children to be perfect; he just wants our devotion, our faith, our obedience.

At times, many of us make excuses to protect ourselves from possible mistakes. We often anticipate failure, which then gives us a reason not to do what God has already equipped us for. Sometimes we make excuses for ourselves and then deceptively believe that they have come from God. This doesn't just apply to not doing something, but also to things that we choose to do. This is why it is so important to develop an ear to hear, so that we gain clarity in our connection with the Lord. We have to get out of the place of self-deception and justification, and get into the place of acceptance and courage in our assignment.

We also make excuses in our journey through purpose because we are afraid of how people will receive us. Moses feared that the people would not receive him because of his lack of eloquence. I would go as far as to say that maybe he did not want to stand out from amongst them. Maybe he was afraid that they would not respect him or hear him. The spirit of rejection is a powerful deterrent in our journey through purpose, and when this spirit is in operation, we often convince ourselves that we are not good enough and others won't receive us well. Have you ever felt led to say something by God, but chose not to for fear of how you would be received? What about that time you made excuses for not speaking up and told yourself and others that no one was going to listen to you anyway? Whenever your thoughts start to sound like this, know that the spirit of rejection is in operation, driving you to make excuses.

When we make excuses for our choices, we deny ourselves the truth and diminish the potential for God to be manifested in our lives. We must be willing to get over ourselves by changing our internal language and gaining the courage to move forward despite our fear. I challenge you to begin to create powerful internal rebuttals for your excuses, and through the act of your will, to proceed forward.

Here are some strategies for getting past your excuses:

- Tell yourself the truth. Refuse to believe the deception triggered by your fear or others' limitations of you. See what God sees and believe in you and God. Seek God. Admit your fears, but don't be defined by them. Embrace your weaknesses and frailties. It's okay if you're not the best at what you're doing. Remember that the Holy Spirit lives within you. Practice, get better, and trust in God for the increase in your life. He gives us all we need for the journey. We just have to get started.

- Own your journey. Take responsibility for your life by controlling what you can and leaving the rest for God to work out.
- Make commitments to your M.O.V.E.ment and uphold them. Implement your will and gain discipline. Daily choose to silence the negative self-talk that enables excuses.
- Choose not to compare yourself to others or to believe that you're not necessary. I struggled with this myself, feeling that there was already enough out there, that I was not needed. But if God has told you to do something, it's obvious that he desires your uniqueness. I don't care if a thousand people do what you do. Ask God what makes you different if you don't know.
- Find your voice, find your impact, find your lane. Don't be afraid to be different or to stand out.

I challenge you today to put away your excuses and to get in the rhythm of God in your life. Get in alignment with God's plan and thoughts of you. I guarantee you, once you embrace them, you become unstoppable.

The Power of the Follow-Through

One of the things I have learned in my life is that it is easier to follow through on our commitments when we have others to be accountable to – we often struggle to be accountable to ourselves. However, in order to obtain our dreams and goals, we must gain the courage to honor our commitments to ourselves despite the challenges and obstacles. I believe that we are in the time of the great rising of God's people. But it is so important in our journey through purpose to be willing to do what we say we are going to do. It sounds easier than it is, but guess what? It's doable.

Doing what we say we are going to do enables us to gain belief in ourselves and the courage to M.O.V.E. forward in our lives. People tend to focus on the accolades, accomplishments, and achievements that come when we complete a goal, and they are good, but who are we becoming in the process? Who we become in our journey through purpose is most important to God and should be to us as well.

When was the last time you made yourself a promise and did not fulfill it? What was it? *I am not going to call that person anymore, I am going to start exercising, I am going to start that business. January 1, I am going to get my business incorporated, I am going to start that ministry, I am going to look for that job, I am going to talk to them tomorrow, next time I won't do this...* The list can go on and on. These broken promises that we accumulate in our lives hinder us from growing and prevent us from operating in the level of faith that is required to finish a thing. But all we need to do is get started, and with faith and the fruits of the spirit, we are able to follow through to completion.

So many of us are known as men and women of our word. When we make commitments to others, we follow through – we are on time, we meet deadlines for our jobs and ministry leaders. There is a drive to not let people down. We have no problem dropping what we are doing to serve our natural and spiritual leaders, yet we fail when it comes to showing up for ourselves. We can gain the courage and faithfulness to honor our commitments to ourselves by taking that first step. Getting started is all.

In my life, I have made it a practice not to mention doing something unless I am willing to see it through. If I don't think I can do a thing or that I have the discipline to complete it, I rarely communicate it or say it aloud. Why? Because once I say it, I become accountable to what I say. A word of caution, though: there is a negative side to this for me. Sometimes I intentionally don't say something just because I don't want to commit to doing it. This means sometimes I am avoiding accountability to things that maybe

I should do. This is an instance in which a system I have put in place to keep me in M.O.V.E.ment can sometimes hinder my follow-through instead. Always be on the lookout for areas where your systems are not supporting you the way you want them to!

When we break our commitments to ourselves, it has the potential to result in inertia. According to techtarget.com, *inertia* is defined as "a tendency to do nothing or to remain unchanged... Inertia is a property of matter that causes it to resist changes in velocity." In our lives, inertia is when we resist change by not following through with our word to ourselves.

How do you feel about people who break promises to you? How is their credibility? When someone doesn't show up for you the way they have promised, you start to look at them as an *untrustworthy person*. These behaviors begin to reveal their character, right? If we can be honest, don't we do the same thing to ourselves? Yes, and over time we start to interpret our behaviors to mean that we can't do it, we won't follow through, we aren't good enough. We become stuck; we get to a place where we have broken so many promises or commitments to ourselves, we even stop trying. This is unhealthy, and we must challenge ourselves to stop this behavior. Yes, we can always change these behaviors, always, but it becomes more difficult once the idea that we are unreliable starts to become a part of our belief system about ourselves.

We must get to the point where we are willing to honor our commitments to ourselves and be intentional about holding ourselves accountable to what we say, and also to what we should be doing – meaning, to what God says. Following through helps us to show up for ourselves, and it always inspires us to keep accomplishing a goal. I challenge you to get to a place where you are just as adamant about keeping your word to yourself as you are about keeping your word to others. Self-accountability!

Do you consider yourself a man or woman of your word? Do people see you as dependable, and even say things like, "If you say you are going to do something, you are going to do it"? I'm sure they do. But I challenge you to get to the point where, in secret, you can say this to yourself.

As we begin to posture ourselves to become better at keeping our commitments to ourselves, I want to make sure that we are realistic in our expectations of ourselves. Ask yourself:

- **Is there a problem with the commitment?** Do I have the capacity? Is this really what I want, or is this what I think I am supposed to do? Am I trying to please another person, rather than God? Sometimes, we don't know what we want, and consequently we do something because it is the right or popular way – but that does not necessarily mean it is *our* way.
- **Is there a problem with me?** Am I mature enough for this commitment? Sometimes we don't follow through on commitments because we aren't mature enough. Am I trying to be something I am not? Do I have something to prove? What is my motive?
- **What needs to change?** What do I need to remove from my way of thinking? What are the barriers to my follow-through? What are the strongholds? Do I have to change my environment, location, and/or relationships? Do I believe in myself? Do I need to gain more faith in God? Do I need to think through things some more before making a commitment?

By thinking about these things, you can begin to identify the changes that will transform the way you look at yourself and allow you to follow through on your commitments.

Follow-through, grit, and commitment are essential in our M.O.V.E. ment. All through this book, a common theme is the need for people to be committed to carrying out the dream and/or assignment of God. Our character and willingness to work must be our guiding forces as we execute the plan of God for our lives. To *execute* is "to put a plan into effect," according to Oxford Languages. We must execute the plan of God for our lives by being consistent in all things and demonstrating the courage to see the plan through to fulfillment.

CHAPTER 9

LIVING OUR M.O.V.E.MENT

"Life is God's gift to us. What we do with it is our gift to God." – A. R. Bernard

The above quote describes for us our responsibility as spirit-filled believers to be good stewards of the gift of life that God has given us. I noted earlier that what we do daily in our lives is a form of worship to our heavenly father. Do you believe that your life, lived out, is a form of worship?

Our ability to M.O.V.E. daily is a direct result of us activating our voice, our vision, and the victory that God has given us. We have a promise from God that declares our victory. As spirit-filled believers, we were sent to earth as gifts to carry out God's plan. Through the Holy Spirit that lives in each of us, we have all the spiritual blessings and resources we need to manifest his kingdom on earth. It is our intentionality and willingness to live according the word of God that will enable us to bring heaven to earth.

Bringing heaven to earth simply means using all of God's infinite resources, creativity, and wisdom to bring healing and restoration to the world. This includes each one of us becoming a conduit of his glory in every part of the earth. Whether in business, arts and entertainment, government, education, health and wellness, spirituality/religion, or family life, we are his conduits, vessels used to demonstrate his power on earth.

Our decision to M.O.V.E. daily by activating our voice, carrying out the vision, and understanding our victory will transform our lives and the lives of all those we touch. We have been given a mandate by God to M.O.V.E. But God did not just give us our order of commission – he has also equipped us with all we need to execute it.

The Power of Our Voice

The voice is a pivotal way for an individual to connect with, understand, and express who they are to others. Connection and expression are the driving forces in our journey through purpose, because ultimately we need them both to share God's plan that is working through us.

In their article "Understanding the Power of Your Voice," Mayra Martin Ganzinotti and Kate Stewart write, "The voice is the muscle of the soul. The voice is our most powerful instrument and has the greatest capacity to generate energy change and stimulate mental processes. There are many aspects of our voice that say much more than the content of our spoken words, making the people who listen to us feel, interpret or trust more, or less, in what we say. Learning about how our voice works and what happens to us when a voice is blocked or broken allows us to get to know each other in a deeper way, and thus be better equipped to face life's challenges with an attitude that is both positive and more real. Your voice is sound, it is an instrument that used consciously can reveal not only the present moment of your being, it can also reveal and support the healing of one's past conditioning and problems affecting them." So from this we understand and can agree with Proverbs 18:21 (AMP), which says, *"Death and life are in the power of the tongue, and those who love it and indulge it will eat its fruit*

CHAPTER 9: LIVING OUR M.O.V.E.MENT

and bear the consequences of their words." Our voice has the ability to change, heal, transform, mobilize, and activate both ourselves and others.

Often when people have experienced trauma, their voice is one of the first things that is diminished. We often feel that what we say doesn't matter, and it forces many of us to devalue our voices. As we journey through purpose and discover the need to heal in this area, one of the first things that is restored in our process is our voice – the courage to speak and to tell our stories. Telling our stories is a powerful tool for healing and restoration. The Bible says in Revelation that we are overcome by the blood of the lamb and the word of our testimony. It is our voice that is the vehicle for deliverance and we must begin to embrace it like never before.

Valuing our voice has everything to do with us respecting and honoring the God in us and seeing ourselves as the vessels through which God desires to speak. Even for those spirit-filled believers who have a speaking gift, it can often be a challenge to believe that what they have to say is important and will be valued by others. This causes most people not to speak, and they find themselves hiding through their silence. Another hindrance is when we are being silenced because of someone else or our thought that they may not want us to speak. How many times have you felt compelled to say something, but because of these thinking patterns, you chose not to? Maybe you felt that you did not possess the authority to speak; maybe you felt that another person would be more eloquent; maybe you even thought that you have done so much wrong that you are unworthy. Maybe you felt that the listeners would not receive you, or that they did not respect you. All of these feelings and thoughts, I can safely say, many of us have experienced. These thoughts and belief systems muzzle us. *Muzzles* are instruments that restrain our normal expression. Our ability to express ourselves has been hindered by our own fears and what others think. I challenge you to begin to examine your voice. Examine your level of expression and ability to connect.

The Bible has so many accounts of God instructing his servants to open up their mouths to proclaim his word. In Isaiah 58:1 (AMP), he told the people to ***"cry aloud and spare not to lift up thy voice as a trumpet in Zion."*** He tells his people to lift their voices, to rejoice. In all these instructions, he is leading his people to use their voices to proclaim, restore, warn, or strengthen the faith of his people. As spirit-filled believers, it is crucial that we understand that our voices are a gift that was meant to be shared with the world. This gift that God has given each of his children can be used for good or evil. It can be used to build or tear down. It can be used to edify or curse. It is essential that we become good stewards of this gift and monitor its usage. I challenge you to consider how are you using your voice. Do you know the power contained in it? What is stopping you from using your voice?

The answers to all of these questions are crucial to our spiritual growth and development and our ability to step into our God-given purpose and assignment on earth. Here are some ways that you can begin to activate your voice in your journey through purpose:

1. Find your unique sound by seeking God and assessing your strengths. Oftentimes, we don't find our own true voices because we spend too much time attempting to sound like others. We attempt to mimic the sounds of others, and we also assume someone else's platform or conviction. Having an intimate relationship with God enables us to discover our uniqueness. Being too entrenched in the convictions of others has a way of diminishing our ability to discover and even value our own voices.

2. Be clear and demonstrate confidence in the use of your voice. Speak... speak...speak and have something to say. The value of your voice is not about the quantity of your words but their quality. What do you have to say, and to whom are you speaking? This matters. Sometimes

we are not able to master our voices because we are too busy trying to be heard rather than effecting change through the power that our voices carry. But we must hold a deep conviction of what has been given to us and be good stewards of it. If you don't know what that is yet, seek him, get in your word, and become an expert in the subject matter you are assigned.

3. Be willing to express your conviction. Know who you are and what your conviction is. People can't distinguish your personal voice until you own and embrace it, until you are able to articulate it with passion. What is your conviction? What is the vision for your life, and what kind of impact do you have with your voice? Can you easily articulate your answers to these questions?

4. Be okay with being set apart. Sometime the power of your voice will cause you to take a stand in controversial matters. It may require you to speak against history or practices that are rooted in traditions, whether in ministry, the community, or the marketplace, and you may have to say things that are not popular. When we value our voices and we understand our responsibility, we must be willing to speak things that go against the grain. In the Bible, God uses his prophets and servants to convey difficult messages. Some attempted to avoid, run from, or taint the word that was given them for fear of the people. We must understand that our voices contain words of wisdom, warning, and wonder. We cannot be willing to speak wonders and not warnings.

5. Commit to spending time in God's presence. Read his word, spend time in prayer, and be intentional in communing with God. Develop a sensitivity to hear his voice and his commands, then obey. It's okay to wait until you hear clearly.

6. Don't be ruled by fear and rejection. Don't be preoccupied with whether you will be received. Just say what you believe is right and what you believe is the will of God for you to say.

These are just a few of the many tips that are helpful in finding the power of your voice. While we have talked about this from the perspective of a spirit-filled believer, it is important for us to understand that the power of our voices is activated wherever we are, whether on our jobs, in our businesses, in our families, or in our communities. God has given us the power to influence through our voices. I urge you to find your place and sound off.

The Power of Time

Time is one of the most invaluable resources that we will ever have. Although we have faith that we have a lot of time, the truth of the matter is that none of us will ever really know how much time we have unless God reveals it to us supernaturally. Time is the beautiful thing that God gives us to grow, to develop, to perfect, and to reconcile back to him.

Often, we take the time that we have been given for granted by demonstrating idleness and entertaining distractions. These things hinder us from steady movement and cause delays and detours. We must look at the time we've been given as precious, a gift that God gives us here on earth. Each of us has an appointed time to be revealed. In Ecclesiastes 3:1 (AMP), it says, *"there is a season (a time appointed) for everything and a time for every delight and event or purpose under heaven."* This scripture has helped me to understand that only God himself has the specifics on when each of these things will happen. God controls our time, yet he gives us the free will to use it, even if that means misusing it.

Do you ever think about how each of us gets the same amount of time in a day? Now I know many of us have differing responsibilities, capacity levels, and levels of focus that can be defined by who we are and what we have experienced in our lives. But how many of us can actually say that we make the most out of the time that is given to us each day? If you are like me, you will easily say no, I have some work to do. Do you think that there is such a thing as stealing time from yourself?

Too often we steal time from ourselves by procrastinating, through avoidance, and by allowing distractions to hinder our movement. We often become consumed with meaningless behaviors and habits that rob us of our productivity. Social media, fruitless activities, depleting relationships that take more from us than they give – these are easy ways to rob yourself of your time. I have done it too often. An hour or two has gone by and you have been stuck on Instagram and Facebook, and then you think, *I could have done my chores, I could have written that paper, I could have finished that proposal, I could have studied my Bible, I could have written that chapter or those pages in my book.* What are other things that take up your time that are fruitless and a distraction to you? Begin to check yourself. Check the time wasters in your life that are robbing you of your destiny and paralyzing your M.O.V.E.ment. There is power in our time, because as long as we have it, we have access to God's infinite imagination to be creators.

Psalm 90:12 (AMP) says, **"So teach us to number our days, that we may cultivate and bring to You a heart of wisdom."** I believe that this is an instruction in the word of God for us to value the time we have and to seek wisdom so that we may be able to make the most out of our days. To number our days implies being intentional about each day and making sure that we are moving within the rhythm of God and living our lives to the fullest. What do I mean by "the rhythm of God"? I believe that each of us has a prescribed time and course that God has ordained and he has divinely orchestrated the events in our lives to bring it to pass. Job says in Chapter 14:5 (AMP), **"Since his days are determined, the number of**

his months is with You [in Your control], and You have made his limits so he cannot pass [his allotted time]." Does this mean that we do not have free will? No. We all have free will with our time. But none of us has the power to stop time. This is why it is so important to get in the frequency of God's timing for your life, so that you can experience the fulfillment of God's plan.

While we cannot stop the flowing of our time, we can choose to make the most out of the time that we have. Often our time is sucked up with busy work, distraction, and noise, but when God's people are able to experience time without disruptions, we gain clarity in our thoughts and more precision in our daily movements, and more importantly we become more aware of our internal and external worlds. Time is a gift and resource given by God, and we must honor it daily.

As spirit-filled believers, we have the power to live supernatural lives. Let's look at ways in which we can maximize our gift of time, using the acronym TIME.

T – To *transcend* is to go beyond the range or limits of something. Let's make the most out of each day and live them out to the fullest. Go beyond what we believe our natural selves can accomplish by tapping into the power that resides within us to fill our days in purpose. It's clear that our natural strength is limited, but when we tap into our supernatural strength, there is no telling what we can accomplish in a day.

I – Be intentional about how your day is spent. To be *intentional* means to do things on purpose, to be deliberate. Be deliberate about your days. Be clear on what you want to accomplish. This doesn't mean you should be a robot, but start your day laser focused and diligent in your behaviors and thoughts. When we are intentional, we are calculated. Operating in wisdom and prudence enables us to get more accomplished and prevents us from being wasteful.

CHAPTER 9: LIVING OUR M.O.V.E.MENT

M - I challenge you to **m**anage your activities to ensure productivity and fruitfulness. To *manage* means to control, influence, or take charge. Take charge of the gift of time each day by not letting it slip away from you. It is so easy to look up and realize the time has gone.

E - To *execute* is to carry out fully. Carry out the tasks and assignments you are set daily. Bringing execution is simply doing what you say you are going to do, being where you should be, and participating in the activities that you need to participate in to accomplish whatever goal you have for that day. Commit to performing.

You might be thinking, *I am not disciplined or consistent enough. I try and just fall right back into a cycle of procrastination*. My challenge to you is to harness the power of time and get back up and go for it again. None of us knows when our time will run out, so it is up to us to keep at it until our lives are emptied according to God's plan for them.

Managing Time on Purpose

Managing time is essential as we journey in our assignments because we often become consumed by distractions that lead to detours from our purpose. We must gain clarity about where God is leading us in every season of our lives and be unyielding in our attempts to move forward as he has ordained for us. But we allow things in our lives to compete against God's plan. This may sound harsh, but it is real. We often get caught in a cycle of doing good things in the wrong seasons and for the wrong reasons.

Are you competing against God's will for your life with your robust schedule? Do your personal, spiritual, and professional pursuits conflict with God's plan for your life? Do you feel overwhelmed by your responsibilities to the point where you don't have the energy to pursue your dreams and goals? Are you sure of what God is doing in your life now? Are you able to distinguish between a good thing and a God thing? All of these questions are very important to consider as you choose to serve God as a spirit-filled believer.

So often in life, we find ourselves feeling overwhelmed by our responsibilities and obligations. We become burned out and can lose direction and our focus on what's really important. We find ourselves experiencing apathy and indecision. It is in these times that we gain a greater appreciation for the management of time and being diligent in stewardship of it. The truth is, time does run out for each of us, and so we must be intentional about our M.O.V.E.ment.

Psalm 90:12 (LBT) says, *"Teach us to number our days and recognize how few they are; help us to spend them as we should."* We must be good stewards of our time. As a therapist, I often help people to identify healthy time management strategies, but truth be told, time management can only flow from a healthy sense of perspective on our priorities and a willingness to be disciplined. As a spirit filled-believer, I believe that time management must also flow from a desire to please God through our obedience.

Managing time runs deep. It is not just about goal setting and accomplishing tasks. It can also be about what you are thinking, what you are feeling, and the nature of your relationships. The Bible says in Ephesians 5:16 (AMP), *"making the very most of your time [on earth, recognizing and taking advantage of each opportunity and using it with wisdom and diligence], because the days are [filled with] evil."*

We get wrapped up in things that rob us of our focus. When we do, we often to experience hindrances and detours as a result. Consumed by our thoughts and feelings, we are disarmed and stuck in the limitations of our soulish realm. This is real and often inevitable when we are involved in relationships with others – relationships are bound to have their difficulties, and when they do, some of us get lost in them. How many times have you thought about something day and night? Have you experienced difficulty in a relationship and been unable to think about anything else? If I tell the truth, it has happened to me many times. When you are stuck in your head and heart, it robs you of the ability to focus on your assignment and the things that are important to God. This is why it is so important to be careful of our connections, commitments, and convictions.

Managing time in our journey through purpose requires us to be good stewards over our three-part being, over our soul, body, and spirit. We are triune beings and each area must be stewarded daily.

This is not just about goal setting and organizing your day to manage your time. This is about examining your life and beginning to remove the people, tasks, obligations, and even good deeds that rob you of your focus in your journey through purpose. It's about putting a stop to avoidance. Many of us fill our schedules with so-called good and righteous things because secretly we are avoiding that thing God has told us to do. I know you are serving weekly in the ministry and doing some amazing things in your community. But answer this – are you doing what God has called you to do?

Managing our time requires the people of God to be more intentional about our endeavors. The Bible says that our steps are ordered by the Lord. It says that we are to seek first the kingdom of God. These instructions require us to make God the priority. Making God our priority may require the sacrifice of our agendas and desires. Can you handle this?

When we do the inner work to manage our focus and our time, we often find we experience more joy and fulfillment following God's instruction than we would have doing our own thing. Our true capacity lies in what we were created for, not always in what we take on. This is not to say that through his amazing free will that he gives us, he won't allow us the grace to do things we want to do. But always remember, God's true investment is in the completion of his will in our lives.

M.O.V.E.ing through purpose is active. It's deliberate, it's part of daily life, it's not theoretical. It's about making a conscious decision daily to maximize your life and potential with wisdom, strategy, and commitment.

Conclusion

As a clinician and minister of the gospel, I have come across hundreds of men, women, and children full of potential and promise. Many of them I have been afforded the ability to see through the eyes of God, and oh my God, the power that is in them is limitless and often mindboggling. But what I find more often than not is they have no knowledge of their own greatness. I can identify with this – for so long, I lived in a diminished reality and was unable to see the greatness in myself. I was unable to recognize my value, and therefore my life and actions reflected a young girl and later a woman who did not love or value herself.

Courage to M.O.V.E. is a book designed to encourage, equip, and empower the people of God with powerful wisdom and strategy guaranteed to propel you to slay the giants in your life. Those giants come from generational sins, personal acts of disobedience, and the traumas of our past. Many of us had no control over the painful experiences in our lives. We didn't get to pick our family, and some of the things that happened to us on the job or in our ministries or communities were completely beyond our control, I know. But still, it is now our responsibility to overcome them. We must fight to M.OV.E.

We must develop an indomitable desire to shed the weights that have beset us and choose a new life. Choosing life requires the sacrifice of our pain and victimhood, which may have become very much a part of our identity, and embrace acceptance, truth, and forgiveness. Although painful and often very difficult to attain alone, we must attain our new identity in Christ so that we can embark upon our pursuit of freedom. Everything that you have gone through, whether good, bad, or indifferent, God can use to deepen your faith and character and create a masterful work of art for his kingdom, *if* you let him.

My prayer is that this book will help you on your journey to the abundant life that God has for you. In this book are powerful strategies that require execution in your daily life. And you do not have to take this journey alone. It is okay to ask for help in your journey through purpose. There are so many therapists, coaches, and spiritual leaders whom God has raised up to be a part of the healing process of his people. These are his gifts that he has sent to earth to manifest his love and power. I challenge you to open up and trust God enough to partner with his people in your process of healing.

Thank you so much for taking the time to read this book. My deepest prayer is that you have cultivated the courage to maximize your moments, overcome your objections, learn to value your vision, and embody your extraordinary.

It's time to RISE AND SHINE!

Scripture References

Preface

Romans 8:28 (TPT): *"So we are convinced that every detail of our lives is continually woven together for good, for we are his lovers who have been called to fulfill his designed purpose."*

Chapter 1

Ephesians 2:10 (AMP): *"For we are His workmanship [His own master work, a work of art], created in Christ Jesus [reborn from above— spiritually transformed, renewed, ready to be used] for good works, which God prepared for us beforehand [taking paths which He set], so that we would walk in them, living the good life which he prearranged and made ready for us."*

Chapter 2

I Thessalonians 5:18 (AMP): *"In every situation [no matter what the circumstances] be thankful and continually give thanks to God; for this is the will of God for you in Christ Jesus."*

I Timothy 6:6 (AMP): *"But godliness actually is a source of great gain when accompanied by contentment [that contentment which comes from a sense of inner confidence based on the sufficiency of God]."*

Romans 12:15 (AMP): *"Rejoice with those who rejoice [sharing others' joy] and weep with those who weep [sharing others' grief]."*

Ephesians 4:29 (MSG): *"Watch the way you talk. Let nothing foul or dirty come out of your mouth. Say only what helps, each word is a gift."*

Hebrews 11:1 (AMP): *"Now faith is the assurance (title deed, confirmation) of things hoped for (divinely guaranteed), and the evidence of things not seen [the conviction of their reality—faith comprehends as fact what cannot be experienced by the physical senses]."*

Chapter 3

I Corinthians 13:4–7 (TPT): *"Love is large and incredibly patient. Love is gentle and consistently kind to all. It refuses to be jealous when blessing comes to someone else. Love does not brag about one's achievements nor inflate its own importance. Love does not traffic in shame and disrespect, nor selfishly seek its own honor. Love is not easily irritated or quick to take offense. Love joyfully celebrates honesty and finds no delight in what is wrong. Love is a safe place of shelter, for it never stops believing the best for others. Love never takes failure as defeat, for it never gives up."*

SCRIPTURE REFERENCES

I John 4:8 (TPT): *"The one who doesn't love has yet to know God, for God is love."*

Psalm 139:13a (ESV): *"For you formed my inward parts; you knitted me together in my mother's womb."*

Jeremiah 29:11 (AMP): *"'For I know the plans and thoughts that I have for you,' says the Lord, 'plans for peace and well-being and not for disaster, to give you a future and a hope."*

Hebrews 10:23 (NKJV): *"Hold fast the confession of our hope without wavering, for he who promised is faithful."*

I Peter 2:9 (AMP): *"But you are a chosen race, a royal priesthood, a consecrated nation, a [special] people for God's own possession, so that you may proclaim the excellencies [the wonderful deeds and virtues and perfections] of Him who called you out of darkness into His marvelous light."*

I Timothy 4:4 (AMP): *"For everything created by God is good and nothing is to be rejected."*

Ephesians 2:10 (KJV): *"For we are his workmanship, created in Christ Jesus for good works, which God prepared beforehand that we should walk in them."*

Romans 14:22 (AMP): *"The faith which you have [that gives you freedom of choice], have as your own conviction before God [just keep it between yourself and God, seeking His will]. Happy is he who has no reason to condemn himself for what he approves."*

Psalm 72:7 (KJV): *"In his days shall the righteous flourish; and abundance of peace so long as the moon endureth."*

III John 2 (AMP): *"Beloved, I pray that in every way you may succeed and prosper and be in good health [physically], just as [I know] your soul prospers [spiritually]."*

Psalm 127:2 (AMP): *"It is vain for you to rise early, to retire late, to eat the bread of anxious labors—for He gives [blessings] to His beloved even in his sleep."*

Proverbs 17:22 (AMP): *"A happy heart is good medicine and a joyful mind causes healing, but a broken spirit dries up the bones."*

John 10:10 (AMP): *"The thief comes only in order to steal and kill and destroy. I came that they may have and enjoy life, and have it in abundance [to the full, till it overflows]."*

Ecclesiastes 3:7 (AMP): *"There is a time to tear apart and a time to sew together, a time to keep silent and a time to speak."*

Proverbs 29:11 (ESV): *"A fool gives full vent to his spirit, but a wise man quietly holds it back."*

SCRIPTURE REFERENCES

James 1:19: *"Let everyone be quick to hear [be a careful, thoughtful listener], slow to speak [a speaker of carefully chosen words and], slow to anger [patient, reflective, forgiving]."*

Proverbs 12:23 (AMP): *"A shrewd man is reluctant to display his knowledge [until the proper time], but the heart of [over-confident] fools proclaims foolishness."*

Proverbs 17:27 (AMP): *"He who has knowledge restrains and is careful with his words, and a man of understanding and wisdom has a cool spirit (self-control, an even temper)."*

Psalm 62:5 (AMP): *"For God alone my soul waits in silence and quietly submits to Him, for my hope is from Him."*

Proverbs 29:20 (MSG): *"Observe the people who always talk before they think—even simpletons are better off than they are."*

John 20:21–22 (AMP): *"Then Jesus said to them again, 'Peace to you; as the Father has sent Me, I also send you [as My representatives].' And when He said this, He breathed on them and said to them, 'Receive the Holy Spirit.'"*

I Corinthians 15:58 (AMP): *"Therefore, my beloved brothers and sisters, be steadfast, immovable, always excelling in the work of the Lord [always doing your best and doing more than is needed], being continually aware that your labor [even to the point of exhaustion] in the Lord is not futile nor wasted [it is never without purpose]."*

Ezekiel 37:5 (AMP): *"Behold, I will make breath enter you so that you may come to life."*

Chapter 4

Psalm 111:10 (AMP): *"**The reverent fear of the Lord** is the prerequisite, the absolute essential, the alphabet of wisdom; a good understanding and a teachable heart are possessed by all those who do the will of the Lord."*

II Peter 1:3 (AMP): *"**For His divine power has bestowed on us [absolutely] everything necessary for [a dynamic spiritual] life and godliness, through true and personal knowledge of Him who called us by His own glory and excellence.**"*

Mark 135–39 (AMP): *"Early in the morning, while it was still dark, Jesus got up, left [the house], and went out to a secluded place, and was praying there. Simon [Peter] and his companions searched [everywhere, looking anxiously] for Him, and they found Him and said, 'Everybody is looking for You!' He replied, 'Let us go on to the neighboring towns, so I may preach there also; that is why I came [from the Father].' So He went throughout Galilee, preaching [the gospel] in their synagogues and casting out demons."*

James 2:14 (ASV): *"**What does it profit, my brethren, if someone says he has faith but does not have works? Can faith save him?**"*

James 2:24 (ASV): *"**You see then that a man is justified by works, and not by faith only.**"*

SCRIPTURE REFERENCES

Proverbs 12:11 (AMP): *"He who tills his land will have plenty of bread, but he who follows worthless things lacks common sense and good judgment."*

Ephesians 2:10 (AMP): *"For we are His workmanship [His own master work, a work of art], created in Christ Jesus [reborn from above—spiritually transformed, renewed, ready to be used] for good works, which God prepared for us beforehand [taking paths which He set], so that we would walk in them, living the good life which he prearranged and made ready for us."*

Psalm 139:13–15 (AMP): *"For You formed my innermost parts; you knit me [together] in my mother's womb. I will give thanks and praise to You, for I am fearfully and wonderfully made; wonderful are Your works, and my soul knows it very well. My frame was not hidden from You, when I was being formed in secret, and intricately and skillfully formed [as if embroidered with many colors] in the depths of the earth."*

Romans 14:12 (AMP): *"So then, each of us will give an account of himself to God."*

Hebrews 4:13 (AMP): *"And not a creature exists that is concealed from His sight, but all things are open and exposed, and revealed to the eyes of Him with whom we have to give account."*

Psalm 37:4 (AMP): *"Delight yourself in the Lord, and He will give you the desires and petitions of your heart."*

Proverbs 16:2 (AMP): *"All the ways of a man are clean and innocent in his own eyes [and he may see nothing wrong with his actions], but the LORD weighs and examines the motives and intents [of the heart and knows the truth]."*

James 1:14–15 (AMP): *"But each one is tempted when he is dragged away, enticed and baited [to commit sin] by his own [worldly] desire (lust, passion). Then when the illicit desire has conceived, it gives birth to sin; and when sin has run its course, it gives birth to death."*

Proverbs 10:17 (AMP): *"He who learns from instruction and correction is on the [right] path of life [and for others his example is a path toward wisdom and blessing], but he who ignores and refuses correction goes off course [and for others his example is a path toward sin and ruin]."*

Proverbs 11:4 (AMP): *"Where there is no [wise, intelligent] guidance, the people fall [and go off course like a ship without a helm], but in the abundance of [wise and godly] counselors there is victory."*

Proverbs 19:2 (AMP): *"Also it is not good for a person to be without knowledge, And he who hurries with his feet [acting impulsively and proceeding without caution or analyzing the consequences] sins (misses the mark)."*

Proverbs 16:3 (AMP): *"Commit your works to the Lord [submit and trust them to Him], and your plans will succeed [if you respond to His will and guidance]."*

SCRIPTURE REFERENCES

James 1:6–8 (AMP): *"But he must ask [for wisdom] in faith, without doubting [God's willingness to help], for the one who doubts is like a billowing surge of the sea that is blown about and tossed by the wind. For such a person ought not to think or expect that he will receive anything [at all] from the Lord, being a double-minded man, unstable and restless in all his ways [in everything he thinks, feels, or decides]."*

James 2:24 (AMP): *"You see that a man (believer) is justified by works and not by faith alone [that is, by acts of obedience a born-again believer reveals his faith]."*

Proverbs 24:15–16 (MSG): *"Don't interfere with good people's lives; don't try to get the best of them. No matter how many times you trip them up, God-loyal people don't stay down long; soon they're up on their feet, while the wicked end up flat on their faces."*

James 1:12 (AMP): *"Blessed [happy, spiritually prosperous, favored by God] is the man who is steadfast under trial and perseveres when tempted; for when he has passed the test and been approved, he will receive the [victor's] crown of life which the Lord has promised to those who love Him."*

Philippians 1:6 (AMP): *"This very thing, that He who has begun a good work in them will [continue to] perfect and complete it until the day of Christ Jesus [the time of His return]."*

Chapter 5

Psalm 31:24 (AMP): *"Be strong and let your hearts take courage, all you who wait for and confidently expect the Lord."*

Philippians 4:13 (AMP): *"I can do all things [which He has called me to do] through Him who strengthens and empowers me [to fulfill His purpose—I am self-sufficient in Christ's sufficiency; I am ready for anything and equal to anything through Him who infuses me with inner strength and confident peace.]"*

II Corinthians 4:7 (AMP): *"But we have this precious treasure [the good news about salvation] in [unworthy] earthen vessels [of human frailty], so that the grandeur and surpassing greatness of the power will be [shown to be] from God [His sufficiency] and not from ourselves."*

Ephesians 6:10 (TPT): *"Finally, be strong in the Lord and in the strength of his might."* / *"Be supernaturally infused with strength through your life-union with the Lord Jesus. Stand victorious with the force of his explosive power flowing in and through you."*

Hebrews 11:6 (ESV): *"And without faith it is impossible to please him, for whoever would draw near to God must believe that he exists and that he rewards those who seek him."*

James 2:17 (TPT): *"So then faith that doesn't involve action is phony."*

Proverbs 18:13 (TPT): *"Listen before you speak, for to speak before you've heard the facts will bring humiliation."*

Colossians 4:6 (TPT): *"Let every word you speak be drenched with grace and tempered with truth and clarity."*

Proverbs 15:1-3 (AMP): *"A soft and gentle and thoughtful answer turns away wrath, but harsh and painful and careless words stir up anger. The tongue of the wise speaks knowledge that is pleasing and acceptable, but the [babbling] mouth of fools spouts folly."*

Galatians 6:9 (AMP): *"Let us not grow weary or become discouraged in doing good, for at the proper time we will reap, if we do not give in."*

Ecclesiastes 9:11 (AMP): *"The race is not to the swift and the battle is not to the strong, and neither is bread to the wise nor riches to those of intelligence and understanding nor favor to men of ability; but time and chance overtake them all."*

I Corinthians 15:58 (AMP): *"Therefore, my beloved brothers and sisters, be steadfast, immovable, always excelling in the work of the Lord [always doing your best and doing more than is needed], being continually aware that your labor [even to the point of exhaustion] in the Lord is not futile nor wasted [it is never without purpose]."*

Chapter 6

Galatians 1:10 (NIV) "Am I now trying to win the approval of human beings, or of God? Or I am trying to please people? If I were still trying to please people, I would not be a servant of Christ."

I John 2:16 (TPT): *"For all that the world can offer us—the gratification of our flesh, the allurement of the things of the world, and the obsession with status and importance—none of these things come from the Father but from the world."*

Matthew 5:16 (TPT): *"So don't hide your light! Let it shine brightly before others, so that your commendable works will shine as light upon them, and then they will give their praise to your Father in heaven."*

Colossians 3:1-4 (TPT): *"Christ's resurrection is your resurrection too... Yes, feast on all the treasures of the heavenly realm and fill your thoughts with heavenly realities, and not with the distractions of the natural realm. Your crucifixion with Christ has severed the tie to this life, and now your true life is hidden away in God in Christ. And as Christ himself is seen for who he really is, who you really are will also be revealed, for you are now one with him in his glory!"*

II Timothy 4:5 (AMP): *"But as for you, be clear-headed in every situation [stay calm and cool and steady], endure every hardship [without flinching], do the work of an evangelist, fulfill [the duties of] your ministry."*

SCRIPTURE REFERENCES

Job 34:21 (AMP): *"For his eyes are on the ways of a man, and he sees all his steps."*

John 7:18 (NIV): *"Whoever speaks on their own does so to gain personal glory, but he who seeks the glory of the one who sent him is a man of truth; there is nothing false about him."*

John 3:27 (KJV): *"A man can receive nothing, except it be given him from heaven."*

Ecclesiastes 3:1 (AMP): *"There is a season (a time appointed) for everything and a time for every delight and event or purpose under heaven."*

I Samuel 16:7 (NIV): *"Do not look at his appearance or at the height of his stature, because I have rejected him. For the LORD sees not as man sees; for man looks at the outward appearance, but the LORD looks at the heart."*

Proverbs 29:18 (MSG): *"If people can't see what God is doing, they stumble all over themselves; but when they attend to what he reveals, they are most blessed."*

John 7:24 (AMP): *"Do not judge by appearance [superficially and arrogantly], but judge fairly and righteously."*

Ephesians 1:18 (TPT): *"The light of God will illuminate the eyes of your imagination, flooding you with light and spiritual sight, until you experience the full revelation of the hope of his calling—that is, the wealth of God's glorious inheritances that is in you."*

Chapter 7

John 3:3 (AMP): *"I assure you and most solemnly say to you, unless a person is born again [reborn from above—spiritually transformed, renewed, sanctified], he cannot [ever] see and experience the kingdom of God."*

John 3:6 (AMP): *"That which is born of the flesh is flesh [the physical is merely physical], and that which is born of the Spirit is spirit."*

Daniel 11:32b (KJV): *"But the people that do know their God shall be strong, and do exploits."*

Philippians 4:13 (ESV): *"I can do all things through Christ who strengthens me."*

II Corinthians 10:4-6 (AMP): *"The weapons of our warfare are not physical [weapons of flesh and blood]. Our weapons are divinely powerful for the destruction of fortresses. We are destroying sophisticated arguments and every exalted and proud thing that sets itself up against the [true] knowledge of God, and we are taking every thought and purpose captive to the obedience of Christ."*

John 10:10 (TPT): *"A thief has only one thing in mind—he wants to steal, slaughter, and destroy. But I have come to give you everything in abundance, more than you expect—life in its fullness until you overflow!"*

SCRIPTURE REFERENCES

Ephesians 3:19–21 (AMP): *"And [that you may come] to know [practically, through personal experience] the love of Christ which far surpasses [mere] knowledge [without experience], that you may be filled up [throughout your being] to all the fullness of God [so that you may have the richest experience of God's presence in your lives, completely filled and flooded with God Himself]. Now to Him who is able to [carry out His purpose and] do superabundantly more than all that we dare ask or think [infinitely beyond our greatest prayers, hopes, or dreams], according to His power that is at work within us, to Him be the glory in the church and in Christ Jesus throughout all generations forever and ever. Amen."*

Proverbs 3:6 (AMP): *"In all your ways know and acknowledge and recognize Him, and He will make your paths straight and smooth [removing obstacles that block your way]."*

Hebrews 11:69 (AMP): *"But without faith it is impossible to please him: for he that cometh to God must believe that he is, and that he is a rewarder of them that diligently seek him."*

Philippians 4:6 (AMP): *"Do not be anxious or worried about anything, but in everything [every circumstance and situation] by prayer and petition with thanksgiving, continue to make your [specific] requests known to God. And the peace of God [that peace which reassures the heart, that peace] which transcends all understanding, [that peace which] stands guard over your hearts and your minds in Christ Jesus [is yours]."*

Ecclesiastes 9:11 (KJV): *"The race is not to the swift or strong but to those who endure to the end."*

Chapter 8

Proverbs 13:4 (AMP): *"The soul (appetite) of the lazy person craves and gets nothing [for lethargy overcomes ambition], but the soul (appetite) of the diligent [who works willingly] is rich and abundantly supplied."*

I Peter 1:13 (AMP): *"So prepare your minds for action, be completely sober [in spirit—steadfast, self-disciplined, spiritually and morally alert], fix your hope completely on the grace [of God] that is coming to you when Jesus Christ is revealed."*

Proverbs 25:28 (MSG): *"A person without self-control is like a house with its doors and windows knocked out."*

I Corinthians 9:24–27 (AMP): *"Do you not know that in a race all the runners run [their very best to win], but only one receives the prize? Run [your race] in such a way that you may seize the prize and make it yours! Now every athlete who [goes into training and] competes in the games is disciplined and exercises self-control in all things. They do it to win a crown that withers, but we [do it to receive] an imperishable [crown that cannot wither]. Therefore I do not run without a definite goal; I do not flail around like one beating the air [just shadow boxing]. But [like a boxer] I strictly discipline my body and make it my slave, so that, after I have preached [the gospel] to others, I myself will not somehow be disqualified [as unfit for service]."*

SCRIPTURE REFERENCES

Hebrews 12:1–2 (AMP): *"Therefore, since we are surrounded by so great a cloud of witnesses [who by faith have testified to the truth of God's absolute faithfulness], stripping off every unnecessary weight and the sin which so easily and cleverly entangles us, let us run with endurance and active persistence the race that is set before us, [looking away from all that will distract us and] focusing our eyes on Jesus, who is the Author and Perfecter of faith [the first incentive for our belief and the One who brings our faith to maturity], who for the joy [of accomplishing the goal] set before Him endured the cross, disregarding the shame, and sat down at the right hand of the throne of God [revealing His deity, His authority, and the completion of His work]."*

Romans 5:3–4 (TLB): *"We can rejoice, too, when we run into problems and trials, for we know that they are good for us—they help us learn to be patient. And patience develops strength of character in us and helps us trust God more each time we use it until finally our hope and faith are strong."*

Exodus 4:10–13 (AMP): *"Then Moses said to the Lord, 'Please, Lord, I am not a man of words (eloquent, fluent), neither before nor since You have spoken to Your servant; for I am slow of speech and tongue.' The Lord said to him, 'Who has made man's mouth? Or who makes the mute or the deaf, or the seeing or the blind? Is it not I, the Lord? Now then go, and I, even I, will be with your mouth, and will teach you what you shall say.' But he said, 'Please my Lord, send the message [of rescue to Israel] by [someone else,] whomever else You will [choose].'"*

Chapter 9

Proverbs 18:21 (AMP): *"Death and life are in the power of the tongue, and those who love it and indulge it will eat its fruit and bear the consequences of their words."*

Isaiah 58:1 (AMP): *"Cry aloud and spare not to lift up thy voice as a trumpet in Zion."*

Ecclesiastes 3:1 (AMP): *"There is a season (a time appointed) for everything and a time for every delight and event or purpose under heaven."*

Psalm 90:12 (AMP): *"So teach us to number our days, that we may cultivate and bring to You a heart of wisdom."*

Job 14:5 (AMP): *"Since his days are determined, the number of his months is with You [in Your control], and You have made his limits so he cannot pass [his allotted time]."*

Psalm 90:12 (LBT): *"Teach us to number our days and recognize how few they are; help us to spend them as we should."*

Ephesians 5:16 (AMP): *"Making the very most of your time [on earth, recognizing and taking advantage of each opportunity and using it with wisdom and diligence], because the days are [filled with] evil."*

SOURCES

Emmons, R. A., & McCullough, M. E. (2003). Counting blessings versus burdens: an experimental investigation of gratitude and subjective well-being in daily life. *Journal of Personality and Social Psychology*, *84*(2), 377.

Beattie, M. (1990). *The Language of Letting Go: Daily Meditations for Codependents* (Hazeldon Meditation Series).

Ganzinotti, M. M., and Stewart, K. (2020). "Understanding the Power of Your Voice." Balance. https://balance.media/power-of-voice/

Blumenfeld, D. (2011). "The 4 'P's' of Birth – The Need to Sync Your Body, Your Baby and Your Mind." Shining Light. https://shininglightprenatal.com/2011/06/18/the-4-ps-of-birth-the-need-to-sync-your-body-your-baby-and-your-mind/

Nixon-Shapiro, E., Collins, T., and Neff, K. (n.d.). "Components of the Birth Process: Nursing." Osmosis from Elsevier. https://www.osmosis.org/learn/Components_of_the_birth_process:_Nursing

About the Author

Ebony is a licensed therapist, author, speaker/trainer, entrepreneur, and minister of the gospel. She is gifted as a preacher/teacher and intercessor in the Body of Christ. Ebony provides mental health counseling to individuals, couples and families. She provides group coaching and training in the areas of mental health, personal development and spiritual development.

Ebony is founder of Triple G Living: God, Goals & Grind, a movement, mindset and mandate to educate, equip and empower people to live "Life on Purpose." Triple G Living is designed to help kingdom believers experience freedom from all forms of bondage and to discover their God-given purpose on earth. It is based on the principles of pursuit of God through discipleship, pursuit of God's vision/assignment and execution of that assignment.

Ebony possesses a deep conviction based on Psalm 115:16: ***"The heaven, even the heavens, are the Lord's: but the earth hath he given to the children of men."*** This verse is the foundation of Triple G Living and roots it in the belief that whether in ministry, the marketplace, business or the community, God seeks to manifest his glory through the lives of his people. We are all ordained to be his **public servants!**

To reach Ebony for more resources or to purchase her books, go to triplegliving.com.

F.I.G.H.T. illustrates God's intention for his people to experience true fulfillment, joy and prosperity in their lives. For years, many of us have served God without satisfaction or fulfillment, not experiencing his unique plan for us. We go through the motions of salvation and redemption, but not transformation and true adoption. This book reveals how and why we only gain our true power when we understand God's heart for us and his desire for us to live an abundant life. *F.I.G.H.T.* takes the spirit-filled believer on a journey of discovering God's idea of flourishing and where the true source of their power, authority and fulfillment lies.

ABOUT THE AUTHOR

G.I.I.F.T.S. explores the heart and mind of God when it comes to his creation. God has divinely engineered each of his children to manifest his glory and be a function of his intellect. As God's children, we are gifts sent to this world to embrace, embody and exemplify his divine nature and essence. Servanthood is the sole channel by which God's divine plan and infinite imagination are revealed on earth. This book takes you on a journey of discovering the spirit-filled believers' true purpose in the world.

This book explores God's intention for prayer, the different types of prayer and the promises God makes to a spirit-filled believer who prays according to the word of God. Through this book, readers will gain a greater understanding of the power that is activated when the spirit-filled believer prays and of the victory which is the divine promise of God. It also includes powerful prayers that will bring hope, strength and encouragement in all aspects of the reader's life.

www.ingramcontent.com/pod-product-compliance
Lightning Source LLC
Chambersburg PA
CBHW050235120526
44590CB00016B/2099